Total Heart Health
for Women Workbook

Total Heart Health for Women Workbook

Achieving a Total Heart Health Lifestyle in 90 Days

Dr. Ed and Jo Beth Young

Michael Duncan, M.D. and Richard Leachman, M.D.

Physical Fitness Expert Kristy Brown

NELSON IMPACT
A Division of Thomas Nelson Publishers
Since 1798

www.thomasnelson.com

Important Caution—Please Read:

The principles and practices recommended in this book result from the research and experiences of the authors. However, the reader is strongly cautioned to consult with his or her personal physician *before* initiating any changes in physical lifestyle. While the Total Heart Health approach has proven effective for many people in improving overall heart health, it is not intended as a strategy for curing serious heart disease. The reader should not use this book as the ultimate source of information about the subject of the book.

This book is sold without warranties of any kind, express or implied, and the publisher and author disclaim any liability, loss, or damage caused by the contents of this book.

Published by Nelson Impact, a Division of Thomas Nelson, Inc., P.O. Box 141000, Nashville, Tennessee, 37214.

All Scripture quotations, unless otherwise indicated, are taken from *The Holy Bible*, New American Standard Bible®, Copyright © The Lockman Foundation 1960, 1962, 1963, 1968, 1971, 1972, 1973, 1975, 1977. Used by permission. (www.lockman.org)

ISBN 1-4185-0127-1

Printed in the United States of America

05 06 07 08 09 — 5 4 3 2 1

CONTENTS

The Total Heart and the 90-Day Challenge

A "New You" in 90 Days

There can be a new you in 90 days! That's the aim of the strategies detailed in this workbook. In *Total Heart Health for Women*, we detailed the meaning and need for Total Heart Health. This workbook will help you understand how to implement your own 90-day plan leading to a Total Heart Health lifestyle.

Meeting this challenge won't just happen automatically. Changing an unhealthy behavior pattern is nothing more than replacing it with a healthy behavior. Some experts in behavior change contend it takes about 21 days to break an existing behavior, 40 days to establish new behavior, and 90 days to transform the new behavior into a lifestyle. While there may be questions about the scientific validity of this idea, many people have found the pattern to be accurate. Getting out of shape physically and spiritually is a process over time, so getting back in shape will take time, too.

Heart disease is a top killer of women, and among the reasons is the fact that when people think of heart health, many don't consider the Total Heart. The assumption is that by caring for one facet of the heart—the physical—the heart will be healthy. But despite dramatic improvements in treating the physical heart, tens of thousands of people still die annually from heart disease.

That leads us to ask: What is the "Total Heart"? Understanding the answer to this question is critical. There can be no genuine Total Heart Health unless the entire heart is considered. There cannot be a "new you" if the totality of your heart is not renewed.

Kitchen and Pantry

Think about a house, one structure with several rooms. If garbage stacks up in one of the rooms, its stench permeates the whole house. On the other hand, if a wall in a bedroom is covered with fresh paint, its odor reaches into other parts of the house.

So, let's consider your heart as a single structure of two major parts—the spiritual and the physical. The spiritual has two facets—the spirit and the soul. Again, let's think about a house. Imagine a country house with a big kitchen. Tucked inside the kitchen is a little room where good things are kept, the pantry. The soul is that dimension of your inner heart that enables you to think, feel, and choose. It is the center of your personality. Right at the core of your soul, like the pantry in the kitchen, is your spirit. This is the aspect of your heart that is capable of communion with God.

Total Heart Health, then, is vitality of the spirit, mind, emotions, and will, as well as physical well-being. Like the happenings in the various rooms of a house, the spirit, soul, and body all interact with one another, affecting your health for good or for bad.

Setting Our Focus: 1 Thessalonians 5:23

Meditate on this passage, and jot down your thoughts about what 1 Thessalonians 5:23 is saying.

_____

_____

_____

_____

Total Heart Health is a lifestyle. The 90-Day Challenge presented here is designed to help you embark on lifestyle transformation. So, it's important to understand your current lifestyle, as well as the changes that need to be made. Take a few moments to work through the Personal Lifestyle Assessment below, and you will gain new insights into yourself.

Personal Lifestyle Assessment

My Spiritual Lifestyle

I give time each day to personal communion with God, involving worship, prayer, Bible reading, and meditation. (Circle the response that best answers the question.)

Always   Sometimes   Rarely   Never

Ways in which I need to change my values regarding personal communion with God:

_____

_____

_____

I am an active member of a Bible-believing church where I am involved with others in worship, learning, and ministry.

Regularly   Occasionally   Rarely   Never

Ways in which I need to change my values regarding the Church:

_____

_____

_____

My Mental Lifestyle

My mind dwells consistently on the characteristics listed in Philippians 4:8: those things which are true, honorable, right, pure, lovely, and of good reputation.

Usually   Sometimes   Rarely   Never

Ways in which I need to change my mental values:

_____

_____

_____

I feed my mind a positive diet through what I read, what I watch on TV, what I see at the movies, and the music I listen to.

Always   Usually   Rarely   Never

Ways in which I need to change my mental diet:

_____

_____

_____

My Emotional Lifestyle

I generally feel peaceful.

Always   Usually   Rarely   Never

Things I can do to align my professed and actual values, reduce my inner conflict, and gain greater peace:

1. _____

2. _____

3. _____

4. _____

5. _____

I usually am joyful in my outlook and emotional experience.

Always   Usually   Rarely   Never

Actions I will take to focus on the values that bring me real joy:

1. _____

2. _____

3. _____

4. _____

5. _____

I react calmly in situations of stress and crisis.

Always   Usually   Rarely   Never

Ways in which I need to change my values in order to remain calm:

_____

_____

_____

I don't get angry easily.

Always   Usually   Rarely   Never

Ways in which I need to change my values to reduce my threshold of anger:

_____

_____

_____

My Volitional Lifestyle

I seek God's will about every decision.

Always   Usually   Rarely   Never

Ways in which I need to change my values regarding God's will:

_____

_____

_____

I give careful consideration to all implications before making a decision.

Always   Usually   Rarely   Never

Ways in which I need to change my values regarding being thoughtful about decisions:

_____

_____

_____

I make choices in line with my principles.

Always   Usually   Rarely   Never

Ways in which I need to change my values regarding my view of principles:

_____

_____

_____

My Physical Lifestyle

Diet

I am conscious of the need to eat a balanced diet.

Always   Usually   Rarely   Never

Ways in which I need to change my values regarding eating a balanced diet:

_____

_____

_____

I watch my calorie intake.

Always   Usually   Rarely   Never

Ways in which I need to change my values regarding my consumption of calories:

_____

_____

_____

Exercise

I give time each day to a physical workout.

Always   **Usually**   **Rarely**   **Never**

Ways in which I need to change my values regarding physical exercise:

_____

_____

_____

Obviously this Personal Lifestyle Assessment is not exhaustive, but it can reveal a great deal about the things you really care about, and around which your lifestyle is shaped. Now we will consider some practical principles for making value and lifestyle changes.

SECTION 2
The 90-Day Total Heart Health Challenge

The 90-day transformation that we present here can be compared to the process of making bread at home—a lost culinary art in many of our homes. There are three stages to the process: sifting, kneading, and baking. The stages of Total Heart Health transformation are also achieved in three stages: the first 21 days, 40 to 45 days, and finally 90 days.

Sifting

When you make bread, you first *sift* the ingredients together to remove the coarser elements and create a new mixture for the bread you want make. *The first three weeks of the Total Heart Health plan will help you sift out old, bad habits and replace them with new, healthy habits.* For example, as you begin to implement the eating plan we recommend, you will let go of the nasty habits of snacking your way through the day or bingeing on sweets, and start eating the right foods in the right quantities. You will be prompted to break away from that couch-potato lifestyle and get into a program of daily exercise. And if a hectic schedule has left you feeling spiritually empty, you will begin carving out time to read the Bible and talk to God in prayer.

After about three weeks of daily practicing healthy physical and spiritual disciplines, you should sense that you have established a positive, healthy, new "groove" for your life.

Kneading

Second, in baking bread, you *knead* the dough. Kneading by hand is hard work—repeatedly pressing, squeezing, and twisting your ingredients into an entirely new entity: bread dough. *During the next three to four weeks of the Total Heart Health challenge, you will work out and fine-tune the good habits you have established.* It can be hard work maintaining the routine and fighting the temptation to fudge a little on your plan. But stick with it.

At about the 45-day point in the 90-day process, your daily health disciplines will take on new meaning to you. You should sense a closer personal connection with God that goes beyond the regimen of just "doing" daily Bible reading and prayer.

Baking

Third, in our bread-making analogy, you *bake* the bread. *During the second half of the 90-Day Challenge, you will look and feel more like the person you want to be than the person you were.* The healthy regimens and routines you have established become your normal, second-nature way of doing things.

We firmly believe that three months after embracing our Total Heart Health challenge, you will look in the mirror and see a new woman!

SECTION 3
Setting Goals for Lifestyle Transformation

This section will help you get started on your Total Heart Health journey. You can't go anywhere if you don't know your destination. Goals identify where you want to arrive. But before you can set goals, you must know where you are. You can't identify the route to your destination if you don't know your starting place. Analyzing our needs tells us what our goals should be, because the goals fill the needs. Objectives are the specific steps we will take to reach the goals that meet the needs.

To determine your Total Heart Health goals, it's important to work through the following section carefully, giving thought to each question. At the conclusion, you will have a set of realistic, attainable goals, with workable objectives that will lead to a transformation of your lifestyle!

Sadly, many of us try to change our lives in spurts. But it doesn't work that way, physically *or* spiritually. Changing behavior is a five-stage process: pre-contemplation, contemplation, preparation, action, and maintenance.[1]

Many models of behavioral change don't succeed because they ignore the fundamental power of change, which is spiritual. Total Heart Health begins with your personal communion with God. Total Heart Health is the linkage of spirit, soul, and body. What happens in your spirit, in its healthy relationship to God, impacts your mind and emotions (soul) and your physical dimension (body).

What follows here is a program you can implement to transform your personal communion with God—which is where all health begins—and improve your mental, emotional, and physical health.

The Facts about My History and Past Practices

In this section, you will be presented sets of questions. Please circle the answers that best describe your experience. Then circle a number that indicates the level of the condition described in the answer. The number 1 stands for the least existence of the condition indicated, and 5 the greatest. For example, if you circle that when you were growing up, your family was "ungodly" to the extreme, you would circle the number 5 under that category.

Spiritual Facts about Me
(Circle and rate the appropriate answers according to the directions given above.)

1. Growing up, my family was:
Ungodly (immoral and openly sinful)

1   2   3   4   5

Occultic (involved in witchcraft, sorcery, astrology, etc.)

1   2   3   4   5

Unspiritual (not interested in God, the Bible, church, etc.)

1   2   3   4   5

Antireligious (perhaps accepting of God's existence, but opposed to and critical of "organized religion" and the Church)

1   2   3   4   5

Irreligious (not opposed to "organized religion" or the Church, but disinterested; not church attenders)

1   2   3   4   5

Somewhat religious (occasional church attenders with a slight interest in spirituality)

1   2   3   4   5

Religious (Church attenders and practitioners of a particular religion, but having little or no real relationship with God)

1   2   3   4   5

Committed Christians (family members serious in following Christ, considering themselves as His disciples, or "learners")

1   2   3   4   5

2. The people who influenced me the most in my early life motivated or inspired me to:
Not believe in God

1   2   3   4   5

Ignore God, if they believed He existed at all

1   2   3   4   5

Rebel against God and His ways

1   2   3   4   5

Be religious

1   2   3   4   5

Become a Christian so I could go to heaven

1   2   3   4   5

Become a Christian and a serious disciple of Jesus Christ

1   2   3   4   5

3. Some of my heroes throughout my life have included the following:

Their names:

_____

_____

_____

_____

Why these people appealed to me:

_____

_____

_____

_____

Important things I learned from my heroes:

_____

_____

_____

_____

4. List the people you knew personally (not family members) who molded your life
   in the past:

Person:

What impact this person made on my life:

_____

_____

_____

Person:

What impact this person made on my life:

_____

_____

_____

Person:

What impact this person made on my life:

_____

_____

_____

Mental and Emotional Facts about Me

1. List one word that would characterize your relationship with the following people
   when you were growing up:

Father: _____

Mother: _____

Brother(s): _____

Sister(s): _____

Aunts/Uncles: _____

Cousins: _____

2. Do a "weather report" on the emotional and mental atmosphere of the home in which you grew up by circling the appropriate response and then reflecting on the associated questions.

Stormy   *Rainy*   *Cloudy*   *Partly Cloudy*   *Sunshine*

How did the atmosphere of your home affect your mind and emotions negatively?

_____

_____

_____

_____

How did the atmosphere of your home affect your mind and emotions positively?

_____

_____

_____

_____

Physical Facts about Me

One of the helpful tools in medical literature for determining when you are overweight is called Body Mass Index (BMI). Years of obesity research have helped us determine a healthy range for a woman's weight in proportion to her height. Simply put, your height is a reliable standard for determining how much you can weigh and still be within the margin of good health.

You calculate your Body Mass Index using the following formula:

- Your weight in pounds

- divided by your height in inches squared

- multiplied by a factor of 703

1. My present weight is _____.

2. My present body mass index (BMI) is _____.

For example, let's calculate the BMI of two women with the same weight. Alicia stands 5' 10" (70 inches) and weighs 170 pounds.

Alicia's height in inches squared (70 x 70) equals 4900.

Her weight in pounds (170) divided by 4900 equals 0.035.

0.035 times 703 equals a Body Mass Index of 24.6.

Barb also weighs 170 pounds but is only 5' 3" tall.

Barb's height in inches squared (63 x 63) equals 3969.

Her weight in pounds (170) divided by 3969 equals 0.042.

0.042 times 703 equals a Body Mass Index of 29.5.

For the record, *overweight* is clinically defined as a Body Mass Index of 25 or greater. *Obesity* is clinically defined as a BMI of 30 or greater, with 40-plus indicating *severe obesity*, also called *morbid obesity*. Numerous studies have shown that a BMI above 25 increases a person's risk of dying early, most likely from heart disease and cancer. Conversely, death rates decline when the BMI approaches the safe range.

Alicia, with a BMI just under 25, is inside the safe range, just short of being overweight for her height. Barb's BMI of 29.5 puts her at the borderline between overweight and obesity and at higher risk than Alicia for heart disease, related problems, and earlier death. The following will help you quickly identify the weight range that is safe for your height.

3. My present blood pressure is _____.

4. I presently spend _____ minutes per day in some form of exercise.

5. My daily calorie intake averages _____ calories. (Keep a log of each meal's calorie count for a week, and then average the total.)

Your Total Heart Health Needs

(Go back through each fact listed above and state it as a need in your own life, as suggested.)

My Key Spiritual Needs

1. _____
2. _____
3. _____
4. _____
5. _____

My Key Mental and Emotional Needs

1. _____
2. _____
3. _____
4. _____
5. _____

My Key Physical Needs

1. _____
2. _____
3. _____
4. _____
5. _____

My Total Heart Health Goals

By this point, you have learned much about yourself. Now it's time to use that information to set realistic Total Heart Health goals and objectives that address your specific needs. Remember, the more you relate your goals to your needs, the more personal the goals will be.

My Personal Spiritual Health Goals

My 90-day goal regarding personal worship of God:

_____

My 90-day goal regarding prayer:

_____

My 90-day goal regarding Bible reading, meditation, and study:

_____

My 90-day goal regarding church involvement:

_____

My 90-day goal regarding personal spiritual service (ministry):

_____

My Personal Emotional and Mental Health Goals

My 90-day goal for improving my emotional health:

_____

My 90-day goal for improving my mental health (worldview, outlook, attitude):

_____

My 90-day goal for strengthening my self-discipline:

_____

My Personal Physical Goals

In 90 days, my goal is:

To weigh _____ pounds. (Weight loss should not exceed 1.5 pounds weekly.)

To have a body mass index of _____.

To have a blood pressure reading of _____.

My Total Heart Health Objectives

Here are the things I will do to reach my goals and advance through the levels of behavioral change:

1. _____
2. _____
3. _____
4. _____
5. _____

Here are the things I will do to reach my spiritual goals:

1. To achieve my personal worship goal, I will:

_____

2. To achieve my prayer goal, I will:

_____

3. To achieve my Bible reading/meditation/study goal, I will:

_____

4. To achieve my church involvement goal, I will:

_____

5. To achieve my spiritual service/ministry goal, I will:

_____

Here are the things I will do to reach my emotional and mental health goals:

1. To achieve my emotional health goals, I will:

_____

2. To achieve my mental health goals, I will:

_____

3. To achieve my self-discipline goals, I will:

_____

Here are the things I will do to reach my physical health goals:

1. Diet: To achieve my weight loss and BMI goals, I will consume
_____ calories per day.
2. Exercise: I will spend _____ minutes per day in a well-rounded workout program that includes cardio, resistance, and stretching exercises.

Now that you've given time to understanding your Total Heart Health needs and set your goals and objectives, you're ready for the "action" level of behavioral change. Let's get started on the 90-day plan!

Action!

Preparing the Spiritual Heart for Action

Spiritual Diet

In a broad sense, our diet is anything we consume to nourish us—including the "feeding" of our spiritual hearts as well as our physical bodies.

Jesus said that He is the "bread of life" (John 6:48). The Greek word for *life* in this verse is *zoe*. The essence of your spiritual heart diet must be the *zoe*-life of Jesus. As we stressed earlier, that means receiving Christ as your personal Savior.

In the Old and New Testaments, Scripture is also described as something to be taken in or consumed. Ezekiel, for example, is commanded to eat the scroll on which God's Word is written (Ezek. 3:1). Taking the Bible into our lives through reading, meditation, and journaling is as important each day as eating physical food.

Spiritual Exercise

For heart health, "energy in," through diet, must be balanced with "energy out," through exercise and work. We can become spiritually obese, just as we can become physically obese. In physical exercise there are three forms of workouts essential for a balanced program: stretching, cardio, and resistance training. A well-balanced spiritual exercise regimen will also have three basic elements:

Worship

We've all heard the old line, "You are what you eat." It's even truer that "you are what you worship." The ancient Canaanites led barbaric lives in which they sacrificed their children to hideous idols. Worshiping the true God revealed in the Bible leads to a healthy lifestyle. He is to be worshiped "in spirit and truth" (John 4:23). This is the balance of the subjective and the objective in our worship. That is, we are to enter into worship with our emotions and our minds. Biblical devotion involves private, family, and public worship.

Bible Reading, Meditation, and Journaling

Physical food enters through your mouth as you eat and goes to your stomach. Spiritual food comes in through your eyes as you read, and goes to your mind. Both physically and spiritually, what you "eat" eventually spreads to every part of your body as nourishment and energy. But food does you no good if you don't swallow it. The same is true spiritually. There are "tasters" who sample a morsel of Scripture and then spit it out. Meditation is a means of "chewing" and "swallowing" what you take in through your eyes. When you meditate on Scripture, you chew on a verse or section by turning it over in your mind. Journaling is the spiritual equivalent of digestion. By writing down thoughts, impressions, and lessons learned from a passage, you take its truths into your life.

Prayer

In some ways, prayer is the spiritual equivalent of breathing. Like pumping air in and out of your lungs, prayer is a two-way operation. You "exhale" as you express the deepest concerns and needs of your spiritual heart to the Father. You "inhale" as you pause and listen for His still, small voice (1 Kings 19:12–13). Throughout the 90-day Total Heart Health Challenge, we will suggest various prayer exercises to help you as you interact with God.

THE "S.E.L.F." PRAYER EXERCISE

S is for Surrender. Paul urged believers to present their bodies to God as a living and holy sacrifice (see Romans 12:1). Surrender doesn't mean you become invisible. Rather, by surrendering to God you put yourself at His disposal to become His highly visible and useful emissary in the world.

E is for Empty. Jesus said, "If anyone wishes to come after Me, he must deny himself, and take up his cross and follow Me" (Matt. 16:24). Self-denial means emptying yourself of anything that could interrupt the flow of God's energy into your life. This is the time to confess sin, weakness, and inadequacy and receive God's forgiveness, according to 1 John 1:9.

L is for Lift. Worship in the Bible is often associated with the physical posture of lifting up to God. The psalms urge us to lift up our voices, our heads, our hearts, and our hands to God in worship and adoration. As you lift yourself up to God, you are in the perfect position to receive the outpouring of the energy you need.

F is for Fill. Ephesians 5:18 commands us, "Be filled with the Spirit." Having surrendered to God's agenda, emptied yourself of every hindrance, and lifted your heart to God in worship, ask the Holy Spirit to fill every dimension of your being.

THE "HAND" PRAYER EXERCISE

We also suggest that you use your hand to help you organize your thoughts as you pray. Each finger will symbolize a specific matter of prayer, like this:

Your thumb represents gratitude. "Thumbs up" is a powerful expression in body language. Because of its positive implications in the language of the body, let your thumb remind you to give thanks to God. As you pray daily, start with the thumb. Let gratitude shape your outlook and prayer.

Your pointer finger represents the need for guidance. Just as you would use your index finger to indicate directions for someone asking you the way to a certain destination, so you need God's guidance in your life. Ask God for sensitivity for yourself and others to recognize His leadership and direction in your life. Mention specific decisions facing you and submit them to His lordship and control.

Your tall finger represents the importance of praying for those in authority. Who are those human beings who have jurisdiction over your life? Let the Scriptures guide you in praying for them. Ask God to provide godly leadership at every level, leaders who will honor and heed Him. Pray for the salvation of specific leaders and for their response to God's will and purposes in their decisions and policy.

Your ring finger represents family and close friends as you pray. As you pray for your spouse, children, parents, and other family members, include such concerns as God's protection, His provision, and the doing of His perfect will in their lives. You might also have friends who are "closer than a brother" (or sister) whom you will want to include in interceding for those closest to you.

Your little finger represents the poor, neglected, oppressed, and abused. As you pray for these people, listen to the Holy Spirit so that you can pray with insight and understanding rather than merely asking for broad "blessings." Also pray for a spirit of generosity for yourself and the Church, and that God's kingdom will be advanced in the lives of people in need.

THE "MODEL PRAYER" EXERCISE

When His disciples asked Jesus to teach them to pray, He gave them a model (Matt. 6). This prototype prayer serves as a good outline for effective communication with God. We recommend that as you move through the 90-day challenge and beyond, you use the Lord's Prayer as a guide, as the following example suggests.

Our Father (Matt. 6:9): Two important themes are contained in these words.

First, when you pray you are not talking to a disinterested "force," but to Father, *Abba*. This term embraces all the love, trust, and intimacy of a small child referring to her daddy.

Second, the word *our* signifies that you live in a family. So, when we pray, we should be conscious of the fact that we are not focused merely on ourselves, but on the context of the whole worldwide family of which we are a part in Christ.

. . .who is in heaven: While God is close to us as Father, He is also above us. "Immanence" means the Father's nearness, and "transcendence" refers to His lofty Being. Right up front, Jesus leads us to understand both of these facets of God's character. Therefore, Jesus wants us to have a balanced view of God's presence and personality as we pray.

. . . Hallowed be Your name: The English word *hallow* comes from the same Greek word as *holy*. It means to recognize that something is set apart, different from everything else. Whatever is "hallowed," or holy, is to be revered and respected.

. . . Your Kingdom come (verse 10): Jesus' second concern is for the advancement of the kingdom of God in the world, and He wants us to identify with this passion for the kingdom.

. . . Your will be done, On earth as it is in heaven: There are no obstructions to the implementation of God's will in heaven. God's kingdom is the rule of God's will; therefore, wherever God's will prevails, His kingdom rules, beginning with our own hearts.

. . . Give us this day our daily bread (verse 11): Jesus gave the specific instruction that we are not to be continually fretting about future needs (Matt. 6:34). Every day we should understand that all we have comes from God's hand, including our ability to earn a living.

. . . And forgive us our debts, as we also have forgiven our debtors (verse 12): When we pray, we need to be specific, listing ways we've come short of God's righteous character and receiving His forgiveness through Christ's grace. However, we should also note that we receive forgiveness in direct proportion to our willingness to forgive others. So, when you ask God to forgive you, think of people who've wronged you, whom you need to forgive.

. . . And do not lead us into temptation (verse 13): Jesus was saying we are to ask God to watch our steps, that we might not wander into a zone of testing and trial. There will be times when God sovereignly allows us to be tested to strengthen our faith and train us for spiritual warfare, but that is in His hands.

. . . but deliver us from evil: Jesus said we are to pray for God to draw us away from and rescue us from everything that would harm us in our totality. Evil harms not only our spiritual hearts, but our physical hearts as well.

. . . For Yours is the kingdom and the power and the glory forever: If we focus on ourselves in prayer without a foundational reverence for God, we become spiritual humanists, self-absorbed and self-worshiping. Much in the model prayer does indeed deal with the self, but there can only be a healthy self-focus in the context of a worshipful God-focus.

Ministry Action

We are to "work out" what we "work in" (Phil. 2:12). Spiritual obesity is an unhealthy condition. Just as its physical counterpart, it comes as we take in more than we expend in exercise and work. Bible reading, meditation, and journaling constitute "energy in"; worship and prayer are means of spiritual exercise; and ministry is work. Exercise and work are the essential in the "energy in–energy out" dynamic. You are most effective when you are ministering through your spiritual gifts (see 1 Corinthians 12), and in that sphere, or area, where you function best (see 2 Corinthians 10).

Preparing the Physical Heart for Action

Diet

In the 90-Day Total Heart Health Challenge, we will propose a dietary regimen designed to help you take off weight and remain healthy. Some diets result in drastic weight loss, but sometimes they can actually be harmful to your physical health. While you are following them, you may slim down and look better, but in the long run, you may be worse off. Our aim is to balance weight loss and health.

The menus we share with you capture the wholesome goodness of common foods in delicious, easy-to-prepare meals. These dishes are rich in fruits, vegetables, and whole grains, making them high in fiber and low in saturated and trans fats. Each daily menu averages approximately 1,300 calories. (Depending on the body weight and current calorie consumption, 1,300 calories may not be appropriate, but can constitute a goal.) The following table breaks down the average distribution of metabolic fuels and other important nutrients.

Total Heart Health Menus

Nutrition Summary
Daily Average of 1,300 Calories

Calories	1348	
Protein	92 grams	28 percent of calories
Carbohydrates	155 grams	46 percent of calories
Fats	40 grams	26 percent of calories
Fiber	25 grams	
Sodium	2500 milligrams	
Potassium	2600 milligrams	

As with all low-calorie diets, however, the Total Heart Health menus may not fulfill all the recommended portions of nutrients according to the National Academies of Science. So we suggest that any adult adopting this eating plan supplement her diet with one multivitamin and 600 mg of calcium daily. These menus are not recommended for children under the age of nineteen.

Our suggested menus provide the weekly amount of omega-3 fatty acids recommended by the American Heart Association by including seafood at least twice a week. However, persons with chronic illnesses such as heart disease and autoimmune disorders should receive 1000 mg of omega-3 fatty acids per day, usually requiring three to five capsules of fish oil supplement daily.

Please note that not all condiments used in these menus are fat-free, most notably the salad dressings. Don't use all fat-free condiments when the meal itself is generally low in fat because nutrient absorption will be negatively affected. A study in the *American*

Journal of Clinical Nutrition revealed that a substantially greater absorption of carotenoids (lycopene, alpha and beta carotene) was observed when salads were consumed with full-fat rather than reduced-fat salad dressing.

The menus recommended here are relatively low in sodium. If salt or salty foods, such as bouillon, are added in the food preparation, daily sodium intake will be higher.

General Menu Guidelines

As you use the menus we provide, here are some important guidelines to keep in mind.

Servings. Unless otherwise noted, these menus are presented in servings for one person. If others in your household are following this plan, simply add additional servings for them.

Eggs. Eggs are a good source of protein, and they are included in several breakfast menus. But eggs should be prepared without fat—they should not be fried in butter! Eggs may be boiled, poached, or fried in fat-free cooking spray. We recommend that you use omega-3 enriched eggs whenever possible, such as Eggland's Best, EggsPlus, or Christopher Eggs.

Bread and cereal products. Whenever the menu calls for bread, toast, crackers, dinner rolls, and the like, we recommend 100 percent whole-grain products that provide at least three grams of fiber per serving. As for breakfast cereals, buy low-fat, whole-grain hot and cold cereals that contain at least four grams of fiber per serving.

Sweeteners. If you wish to sweeten menu items, such as dry or cooked cereal, we recommend a calorie-free sugar substitute.

Spreads. If you wish to add a buttery spread to bread or cooked vegetables, we recommend a butter substitute, such as imitation butter flakes.

Fresh fruit. Whenever a menu calls for "1 piece of fresh fruit," you may use one of the following: 1 medium orange, apple, peach, nectarine, or pear; $\frac{1}{2}$ grapefruit; $\frac{1}{2}$ cantaloupe; 1 cup melon chunks; 2 small plums or kiwis; 1 cup strawberries; $\frac{1}{2}$ cup other berries (such as blueberries, raspberries, blackberries); 1 small banana; 1 cup grapes (freeze them for fun!); or $\frac{1}{2}$ cup fresh pineapple or canned pineapple in its own juice.

Raw vegetables. Whenever a menu suggests a snack of raw veggies, one serving is filled with either two stalks of celery, six baby carrots, one medium green pepper, one medium tomato, or other vegetables in equivalent amounts.

Fish. Whenever a menu entrée features fish, we recommend red snapper, sole, tilapia, flounder, albacore, or salmon. Whenever possible, use cold-water fish instead of farm-raised.

Beverages. No beverages are included in these menus, nor are they included in the daily averages for calorie intake. An important part of a healthy daily diet is water intake—approximately eight 8-ounce glasses per day. Drinking a glass of water with each meal is one way to help you fulfill that need. If you prefer other beverages with meals and snacks, such as coffee, tea, or soda, we recommend sugar-free varieties.

Exercise

A complete exercise program consists of three categories of activity: cardiovascular, resistance, and flexibility. For the best results, combine all three based on your personal fitness needs. Resistance exercises help you with daily activities by developing strength for strenuous tasks such as lifting the kids in and out of car seats, pushing a wheelbarrow while gardening, opening the tight lid on a new jar of pickles, etc. Flexibility exercises will keep you mobile and limber with good range of motion throughout life. And cardio exercises, the most important, are essential for keeping your heart strong and healthy. Let's look at each in detail.

Cardiovascular Exercise for a Stronger Heart

Cardiovascular exercise takes place when you move your large muscle groups rhythmically and repetitively, such as in walking, running, biking, swimming laps, dancing, or stepping. Sustained, repetitive exercise elevates your heart rate, which facilitates blood flow, delivers oxygen to your cells, and increases metabolic rate.

Cardiovascular exercise is always about progression—starting at a safe, comfortable level and periodically working up from there to realize greater benefits. Use the F.I.T.T. scale to guide you as you progress in cardio exercise.

F is *frequency*, how many days a week you exercise.
I is *intensity*, the speed or energy you put into your exercise.
T means the *type* of exercise you do—walking, jogging, stepping, etc.
T is the amount of *time* you exercise each day.

In order to progress, increase your exercise by one F.I.T.T. component at a time. For example, if you swim laps three mornings a week for forty-five minutes, consider lengthening your swim by five minutes each day or adding a fourth morning. If you walk five days a week, you might try increasing the time from thirty minutes to forty minutes, or the intensity from a moderate walk to a fast walk.

Always begin your cardio exercise with a four- to five-minute warm-up and end with a three- to four-minute cooldown. For example, if you jog, warm up with some walking, and then end your jog by slowing your gait and walking. Warm-up allows the heart rate to increase gradually, and cool down brings it back to normal gradually, which is kinder to your heart.

Resistance Exercise for Muscle Tone and Strength

Resistance exercises—also called strength training or weight training—use force on the muscles to strengthen them. Common resistance exercises are weight lifting, working out on resistance machines, and pressing against your own weight, as in push-ups, pull-ups, and sit-ups. The American College of Sports Medicine recommends working all major muscle groups. You have four primary muscle groups in your legs: gluteals, quadriceps, hamstrings, and calves. Your midsection contains two groups: abdominals and lower back. Exercises in this area are very important to good posture because these groups support your trunk and spine. There are five groups in your upper body: pectorals, upper back, shoulders, biceps, and triceps.

We recommend that you work each muscle group with one to three sets of eight to twelve repetitions—or reps—each. The level of difficulty for your resistance program can be measured on a continuum, moving from challenge to fatigue to failure. Start with a challenge and move to the point of fatigue. Those who are more advanced should push themselves past fatigue to the point of failure, meaning they keep lifting until they cannot physically complete a lift.

Flexibility Exercise for Range of Motion

When you stretch properly, muscle fibers get longer. Later in life, range of motion becomes crucial. People begin to notice their bodies tightening at about the age of forty. Aching backs, for example, can often be alleviated with a few minutes of stretching each day.

The American College of Sports Medicine recommends stretching all major muscle groups one to three times per workout session, with one to three sessions a week. The best way to stretch is to extend the muscle and hold it there for ten to thirty seconds. You should feel tension, but not pain. In reality, stretching can be the most relaxing part of your workout. Bear in mind that your muscles don't start on "ready." They need to be extended gently and stretched out gradually.

Your Personal Exercise Routine

Our Total Heart Health recommendation is that, at a minimum, you exercise for thirty minutes a day, five days per week. If you can't start at that level, at least make it your immediate goal.

If general health is your goal, you can vary your exercise during the week. The minimum cardio exercise for general health is twenty minutes a day, three days a week.

In order to build more muscle, exercise a little more than thirty minutes a day, maintaining the three-day cardio and flexibility program while adding ten to fifteen minutes of resistance exercise before or after your cardio. On your two noncardio days, do extended resistance exercises. To achieve muscle growth (hypertrophy), increase your weights and stay on the lower end of repetitions (eight to ten).

In order to lose weight, you must, of course, burn more calories than you take in by eating food. A minimum five-day, thirty-minute cardio exercise is necessary. Initially you may do twenty to twenty-five minutes of daily cardio activity followed by five to ten minutes of stretching. But move up to a full thirty minutes of cardio as soon as possible, and extend that time as your fitness improves. You can do the entire routine at one time or spread your exercise throughout the day. Just be sure to log at least thirty minutes daily. Once you reach that goal, work in at least another fifteen to twenty minutes of resistance exercise.

You must control your intake of calories—energy in—while you burn calories—energy out. When you burn roughly the same amount of calories you eat each week, you achieve energy balance. Once you reach your weight-loss goal, you should adjust energy balance between diet and exercise to maintain your weight.

We recommend a maximum cardiovascular exercise regimen of one hour a day, six days a week. Some people who have become more advanced over time and want to challenge themselves may increase to forty-five minutes of cardio and forty-five minutes of weights in one workout. However, that's not for everybody, and it's not necessary to achieve most goals.

The Bible directs us to take a day of rest each week, and your body needs that rest. When you exercise, your body consumes glycogen, which is the sugar stored in the muscles. Observing an "exercise Sabbath" helps the muscles replenish glycogen stores.

Here's a sample exercise program based on thirty minutes of cardiovascular exercise each day. On days of longer exercise, it's all right to break your regimen into two sections, such as thirty minutes in the morning and thirty minutes later in the day. Always bookend each session with a few minutes of warm-up and cooldown:

Monday	30 minutes of walking followed by stretching.
Tuesday	30 minutes on an elliptical trainer (step machine) and 30 minutes of resistance exercise.
Wednesday	30 minutes of walking, followed by stretching.
Thursday	30 minutes on a stationary bike and 30 minutes of resistance exercise.
Friday	30 minutes on an elliptical trainer.

| Saturday | 30 minutes on a stationary bike and 20 minutes of circuit training (alternating resistance exercises with two to four minutes of cardio movement, such as stepping, walking, cycling, or jumping rope). |

Most people who don't work out at a gym use walking as their primary form of cardiovascular exercise. You can map out a challenging course or two in your neighborhood, perhaps including some hills. Or you may want to walk laps at the local high school gym.

There are cardio alternatives to walking, however. If you have access to a bicycle, use it. Just make sure you're pedaling consistently for the entire ride, because a simple cruise through the park doesn't count for cardio. If you are blessed to live in an area where hiking trails, canoeing or kayaking, or cross-country skiing are readily available, these activities are great alternatives to walking. Another great source for at-home workouts is exercise videos.

You don't need a gym for resistance exercise, either. There are many low-cost exercise tools you can use right in your own home, such as dumbbells and exercise tubing. Here's a sample workout week using home-based devices for cardio and strength training.

Monday	30 minutes of walking, core training, and stretching.
Tuesday	30 minutes of walking or biking and 30 minutes of resistance training using dumbbells or exercise tubing for squats, lunges, bicep curls, crunches, as well as push-ups, sit-ups, pull-ups, etc.
Wednesday	30 minutes of interval walking, meaning to alternate your pace between one minute of fast walking or jogging and two minutes at a more moderate pace. Follow with core training and stretching.
Thursday	30 minutes of walking or cardio workout video and 30 minutes of resistance training with dumbbells, etc.
Friday	30 minutes of walking, core training, and stretching.
Saturday	20 minutes of walking or biking and 30 minutes of circuit training.

When you're ready for a more advanced workout, it might look like this:

Monday	45 minutes of an aerobic class followed by stretching.
Tuesday	30 minutes of fast walking, plus 30 minutes of lifting weights, targeting the upper body.
Wednesday	45 minutes on an elliptical trainer, followed by stretching.

Thursday	30 minutes on a stationary bike, plus 30 minutes lifting weights and resistance training, targeting the lower body.
Friday	45 minutes of kickboxing class, followed by stretching.
Saturday	30 minutes of fast walking or 45 minutes of circuit training.

God designed your body to move, so you should regard exercise as a form of worship to Him. It is a specific way you can honor the temple of the Holy Spirit, your body. Paul urged, "Whether, then, you eat or drink or whatever you do, do all to the glory of God" (1 Cor. 10:31). So exercise to the glory of God and present your body to Him as a "living and holy sacrifice" (Rom. 12:1).

Preparation: "Sifting"

Objective:
To sift out old habits regarding your personal time
with God, and introduce new behaviors.

Guide:
Do the following each day as designated,
for the 21–day period.

Day 1

Remember our bread analogy. "Sifting" is the focus for the first 21 days of the 90-day Total Heart Health Challenge. Follow the suggestions here faithfully. At first they may seem strange, and they will certainly require changes in your daily routine. However, remember that you are "sifting out" old habits and "sifting in" new practices. The more you "sift," the less there is of the old, and the more there is of the new. Don't forget that the aim is to spend thirty minutes per day focused on the spiritual heart, another thirty minutes on exercises that contribute to physical heart health, and eat a heart-healthy diet throughout the day. So stay with it!

Caring for Your Spiritual Heart

Spiritual Energy In

Diet

Bible Reading: John 1:1–18

Meditate on the following questions, and write your answers in the space provided.

1. Compare John 1:1–3 with Genesis 1:3. How are these passages alike?

_____

_____

2. Why do you think the darkness has never been able to overpower the Light?

_____

_____

3. What does it mean to you that Jesus has "pitched His tent" (tabernacled) with us?

_____

_____

Spiritual Energy Out

Exercise

Worship Exercise: Focus your entire worship today on exalting Jesus Christ as the One who is the Source of all being. You might want to use Colossians 1:13–20 as a guide for your worship of the magnificent Christ.

Prayer Exercise: Pray the S.E.L.F. acronym. Come back to the *S* and focus today on "surrender." Surrender each part of your body to God for His use, one by one.

Caring for Your Physical Heart

Diet

Breakfast	1 egg prepared without fat
	1 slice toast with 1 tbsp. peanut butter
	1 piece of fresh fruit
Snack	1 stick mozzarella string cheese
Lunch	4 oz. grilled or baked chicken breast
	Salad with mixed greens and assorted raw vegetables
	1 tbsp. oil and vinegar dressing
Snack	1 piece of fresh fruit
Dinner	4 oz. baked fish fillet: Rub with olive oil, garlic, and other seasoning as desired
	1 cup cooked green beans, seasoned as desired
	1 medium broiled tomato sprinkled with parmesan or goat cheese and other spices as desired
	1 dinner roll
Snack	½ cup instant pudding prepared with skim or low-fat milk
	1 cup strawberries or ½ cup other berries

Exercise Focus for Today

Walking, core training, and stretching.

Two very important elements of your 90-day journey to Total Heart Health are **Physical Energy In** (food and calories consumed) and **Physical Energy Out** (exercise). Because these two elements are so important to your Total Heart Health, we ask you to tear out the perforated page in the back of the workbook specially created to chart your food and exercise for the day.

Make copies of this chart and keep it handy—in your purse or wallet—so that you'll have it readily available to use during the day as you lunch, snack, and exercise. This chart will be vital to the success of your journey, so don't forget to use it!

 **Day 2**

Caring for Your Spiritual Heart

Spiritual Energy In

Diet

Bible Reading: John 3:1–21

Meditate on the following questions, and write your answers in the space provided.

1. Why did Nicodemus conclude that Jesus was a teacher "from God"?

_____

_____

2. Why do you think Jesus uses the analogy of birth to describe coming into relationship with God?

_____

_____

3. Why do you think God's love for the world—including you—meant that He had to give His Son?

_____

_____

Spiritual Energy Out

Exercise

Worship Exercise: Spend a few moments worshiping God for His character of perfect love. Worship Jesus Christ as the expression of that love, and thank Him for sacrificing Himself for you.

Prayer Exercise: Pray the S.E.L.F. acronym all the way through. Return to the *E* and focus on "emptying" yourself of all that stands between you and God.

Caring for Your Physical Heart

Diet

Breakfast Smoothie: Blend 6 oz. silken tofu, ⅔ cup berries, 1 cup apple juice, 1 tsp. vanilla, 1 small banana

Snack Raw veggies

Lunch Tomato stuffed with tuna salad on a bed of greens

Tuna salad: 3 oz. water-packed tuna, 1 hard-boiled egg chopped, 2 tbsp. low-calorie mayonnaise

Snack 1 piece of fresh fruit

Dinner 1 serving beef and broccoli sauté*

½ cup brown rice, steamed or cooked in water or broth

Salad with mixed greens and assorted raw vegetables

2 tbsp. oil and vinegar dressing

Snack ½ cup sherbet

*Beef and Broccoli Sauté (serves 4)

¾ lb. lean beef strips
1 tbsp. olive oil
1 tsp. sesame oil
1 tbsp. soy sauce
½ tsp. red pepper flakes
5–6 cups broccoli pieces
6 cloves minced garlic
2 tbsp. cooking sherry
1½ tbsp. ginger root

Sauté garlic in olive oil, add other ingredients, and cook until meat is done and broccoli is al dente.

Exercise Focus for Today

Resistance training with dumbbells, or push-ups (it's okay to do them on your knees), along with sit-ups or assisted pull-ups.

Don't forget to chart your food consumption and exercise for the day!

 **Day 3**

Caring for Your Spiritual Heart

Spiritual Energy In

Diet

Bible Reading: John 4:1–26

    Meditate on the following questions, and write your answers in the space provided.

    1. What insights do you get into Jesus' personality from His conversation with the woman at the well?

    2. What do you think the woman thought when Jesus began talking to her about "living water"?

    3. What does it mean to you to worship God "in spirit and in truth"?

Spiritual Energy Out

Exercise

Worship Exercise: Use Psalm 8 as a guide for expressing worship to God.

Prayer Exercise: Pray the S.E.L.F. acronym in its totality. Return to the *L*, and praise God for His nature (His lovingkindness, mercy, justice, etc.).

Caring for Your Physical Heart

Diet

Breakfast   2 open-faced turkey-and-cheese melts. On each slice of bread: 1 oz. sliced turkey and 1 slice fat-free cheese. Broil until cheese is melted.

Snack   2 large high-fiber crackers

1 slice low-fat cheese

Lunch   1 serving shredded chicken salad with cranberries,* served over mixed greens

Snack   ½ cup instant pudding made with skim or low-fat milk

Dinner   4 oz. roasted pork tenderloin

½ cup brown rice, steamed or cooked in water or broth

1 cup vegetable medley sauté: Sauté a variety of fresh vegetables (e.g., peppers, onions, squash, snow peas) in olive oil and seasonings of your choice.

Snack   ½ cup fat-free frozen yogurt

*Shredded Chicken Salad with Cranberries (serves 4)

2 boneless chicken breasts, poached until meat falls apart

⅔ cup dried cranberries

3 celery stalks, diced

1 oz. pecans, chopped

Shred poached chicken. Mix ingredients together, toss with dressing, and refrigerate 6–8 hours.

Dressing: In a food processor, combine 2 egg yolks, 2 tbsp. apple cider vinegar, 2 tsp. sugar (or equivalent in sugar substitute), 1 tsp. Dijon mustard. While blending, stream 2 tbsp. olive oil into processor.

Exercise Focus for Today

Interval walking (alternate your pace between one minute of fast walking or jogging and two minutes at a more moderate pace). Follow with core training and stretching.

Don't forget to chart your food consumption and exercise for the day!

 **Day 4**

Caring for Your Spiritual Heart

Spiritual Energy In

Diet

Bible Reading: Psalm 150:1–6

Meditate on the following questions, and write your answers in the space provided.

1. People express praise to God in different ways. What is your favorite style of praising God?

_____

_____

2. Why do you think people sometimes differ in their styles of praising God?

_____

_____

3. Read 1 Corinthians 14. Why would Paul suggest that our style of expression toward God will differ in private and public prayer and worship?

_____

_____

Spiritual Energy Out

Exercise

Worship Exercise: Worship God for His mighty deeds in your life.

Prayer Focus: Pray the complete S.E.L.F. acronym. Focus on the *F*, and ask the Holy Spirit to fill you in your mind, your emotions, your will, and your body.

Caring for Your Physical Heart

Diet

Breakfast	1 cup cereal with skim milk
	1 piece of fresh fruit
Snack	2 lettuce and turkey wraps: Wrap a 1-oz. slice of turkey in each large lettuce leaf.
Lunch	Shrimp Salad: 4 oz. cooked shrimp served with cocktail sauce and lemon juice on a bed of greens
	8 small low-fat crackers
Snack	½ cup low-fat cottage cheese
	½ cup fresh or canned pineapple in its own juice
Dinner	1 roasted Cornish game hen, seasoned to taste
	1 serving braised cauliflower with capers*
	1 medium baked sweet potato
Snack	1 piece of fresh fruit

*Braised Cauliflower with Capers (serves 4)

3 tbsp. olive oil	1 can anchovies, rinsed and minced
3 garlic cloves	¼ tsp. dried red pepper flakes
1 cup water	1¼ lbs. cauliflower florets
3 tbsp. capers	¼ cup parsley, chopped
salt to taste	

Melt anchovies in olive oil over medium low heat, about one minute. Add garlic and pepper flakes, cooking until garlic softens. Add cauliflower and water. Cover and cook seven minutes or until tender. Remove lid; raise heat until water evaporates, leaving a thin layer of juice in bottom of pan. Add capers, parsley, and salt, and serve.

Exercise Focus for Today

Thirty minutes of walking or cardio workout video.

Don't forget to chart your food consumption and exercise for the day!

Day 5

Caring for Your Spiritual Heart

Spiritual Energy In

Diet

Bible Reading: Ruth 1:1–22

Meditate on the following questions, and write your answers in the space provided.

1. What are some positive character traits you see in Naomi?

_____

_____

2. Why do you think Orpah decided as she did?

_____

_____

3. What are the elements of genuine commitment you see in Ruth's statement?

_____

_____

Spiritual Energy Out

Exercise

Worship Exercise: Use Ruth 1:16–17 as a guide to express your devotion to Christ and your willingness to follow Him.

Prayer Focus: Review Question 3. Pray that God will strengthen each of the elements of true commitment to Him in your life.

Caring for Your Physical Heart

Diet

Breakfast   Omelet with 2 eggs with 1 oz. nonfat cheese, 2 oz. turkey, chopped green pepper and mushrooms

1 piece of fresh fruit

Snack   Raw veggies

Lunch   1 cup low-fat, low-sodium soup (e.g., Healthy Choice, Campbell's Healthy Request)

8 small low-fat crackers

Snack   1 piece of fresh fruit

Dinner   Taco salad in baked tortilla bowl*

Snack   1 piece of fresh fruit

*Taco Salad in Baked Tortilla Bowl

4 oz. lean ground beef	1 tbsp. taco spices
½ chopped avocado	½ chopped tomato
2 tbsp. sour cream	1 oz. shredded nonfat cheese
1 whole-wheat tortilla	Mixed greens

Line bottom and sides of ovenproof bowl with tortilla, bake at 350 degrees for 10–12 minutes. Cook beef with taco spices. Fill tortilla bowl with greens; top with meat, avocado, tomato, sour cream, and cheese. And you can eat the bowl!

Exercise Focus for Today

Resistance training with dumbbells, etc.

Don't forget to chart your food consumption and exercise for the day!

 **Day 6**

Caring for Your Spiritual Heart

Spiritual Energy In

Diet

Bible Reading: Ruth 2:1–23

Meditate on the following questions, and write your answers in the space provided.

1. Do you think it "just so happened" that Naomi had a wealthy kinsman who took note of Ruth? Explain your answer.

_____

_____

2. What does this passage tell you about Ruth's personality and character?

_____

_____

3. What insights do you get about Boaz's character from these verses?

_____

_____

Spiritual Energy Out

Exercise

Worship Exercise: Thank God for the people you've listed and the "gleanings" from them that have blessed your life. Begin with Jesus Christ, and what you have "gleaned" from His sacrifice for you.

Prayer Focus: Pray that God will use you to provide "gleanings" for others.

Caring for Your Physical Heart

Diet

Breakfast	1 cup cooked oatmeal with skim milk
	¼ cup dried fruit or ½ sliced banana
Snack	1 piece of fresh fruit
Lunch	Turkey sandwich (2 slices bread, 4 oz. turkey, 1 slice nonfat cheese, lettuce, 1 to 2 tomato slices)
	Raw veggies
	1 oz. pretzels
Snack	6 oz. low-sodium vegetable juice (e.g., V-8)
	2 large high-fiber crackers (e.g., Ry Krisp)
Dinner	4 oz. chicken breast sautéed in olive oil and mixed herbs, such as pulverized basil, parsley, red pepper flakes, and salt
	½ cup sautéed spinach with fresh garlic
	½ cup brown rice, steamed or boiled in water or broth
Snack	½ cup instant pudding made with skim or low-fat milk

Exercise Focus for Today

Combine walking, core training, and stretching.

**Don't forget to chart your food consumption
and exercise for the day!**

 **Day 7**

Caring for Your Spiritual Heart

Spiritual Energy In

Diet

Bible Reading: Ruth 3:1–18

Meditate on the following questions, and write answers in the space provided.

1. Why do you think Ruth trusted Naomi so completely?

_____

_____

2. What does this Scripture passage teach you about how you can build character that the people you love can trust?

_____

_____

3. What do you think were the characteristics people saw in Ruth that caused them to label her a "woman of excellence"?

_____

_____

Spiritual Energy Out

Exercise

Worship Exercise: Read Genesis 22:14. Worship God as your Provider. Think of the "places" in time and space where you would build an altar to celebrate and remember God's miraculous provision for you.

Prayer Focus: What is the provision you need most right now? Ask God for this provision, according to His will, and for the capacity of personal faith for you to receive His provision.

Caring for Your Physical Heart

Diet

Breakfast	2 eggs
	1 slice toast
Snack	1 piece of fresh fruit
Lunch	Chicken salad: Toss together 4 oz. white chicken meat, ¼ cup sliced grapes, 1 tbsp. toasted chopped pecans, 1 tsp. lemon juice, and 1 tbsp. fat-free plain yogurt. Serve on a bed of greens or wrapped in a large lettuce leaf.
Snack	2 oz. pretzels
Dinner	4 oz. baked or broiled salmon marinated in teriyaki sauce
	1 cup vegetable medley sauté (see Day 3)
	½ cup steamed or boiled brown rice, using water or broth
Snack	1 piece of fresh fruit

Exercise: Option—Resting Day, or . . .

Thirty minutes of walking or biking, or thirty minutes of circuit training, alternating cardio with resistance exercise, switching every 1–2 minutes.

Don't forget to chart your food consumption and exercise for the day!

Day 8

Caring for Your Spiritual Heart

Spiritual Energy In

Diet

Bible Reading Ruth 4:1–22

Meditate on the following questions, and write your answers in the space provided.

1. A "redeemer" is a kinsman who has the authority to buy a relative's property and marry his widow. How do you think this idea relates to Jesus Christ being *your* Redeemer?

_____

_____

2. What blessings do you speak regularly upon your loved ones?

_____

_____

3. What important principles does the experience of Ruth and Naomi teach you that will help you when you pass through hard times?

_____

_____

Spiritual Energy Out

Exercise

Worship Exercise: Think about the hard times in your life that God actually used to bring you blessings, and worship Him for His guidance and faithfulness.

Prayer Focus: This week, we will use the HAND strategy for prayer (see page 23). Pray briefly for concerns symbolized by each "finger."

Caring for Your Physical Heart

Diet

Breakfast	Smoothie (see Day 2)
Snack	1 high-fiber granola or protein bar
Lunch	Salmon salad: Toss together 3 oz. leftover teriyaki salmon (or canned salmon), mixed greens, and 2 tbsp. fat-free salad dressing.
Snack	1 slice toast with 1 tbsp. peanut butter
Dinner	4 oz. veal scallopini cooked in olive oil, lemon juice, and white wine, if desired
	1 cup steamed asparagus with lemon juice
	Mixed green salad with ½ sliced tomato
	2 tbsp. vinaigrette salad dressing
Snack	1 frozen fruit juice bar

Exercise Focus for Today

Walking, core training, and stretching.

Don't forget to chart your food consumption and exercise for the day!

 **Day 9**

Caring for Your Spiritual Heart

Spiritual Energy In

Diet

Bible Reading: John 10:1–21

Meditate on the following questions, and write your answers in the space provided.

1. What are some of the things the devil has stolen from you at various points in your life?

_____

_____

2. How has the devil robbed you of good health?

_____

_____

3. Why do you think receiving Christ into your life can make you healthier?

_____

_____

Spiritual Energy Out

Exercise

Worship Exercise: Read through John 10:1–21, and note the positive characteristics of a "good shepherd." Give worship to Jesus for having all of these attributes.

Prayer Focus: As you pray through the HAND model this week, focus today on the thumb, which represents gratitude. Think of specific ways Jesus has been a Good Shepherd to you, and give Him thanks for each.

Caring for Your Physical Heart

Diet

Breakfast 1 whole-wheat pita stuffed with 2 scrambled eggs and 2 oz. nonfat shredded cheese

Snack 1 piece of fresh fruit

Lunch 1 cup low-fat cottage cheese with 1 cup fresh or canned pineapple in its own juice

1 roll

Snack 1 piece of fresh fruit

Dinner 1 serving chicken fajita salad and rice*

Snack ½ cup sherbet

*Chicken Fajita Salad and Rice (serves 4)

1 lb. chicken breast strips	Fajita (or taco) seasoning
1 sliced onion	1 sliced green pepper
1 cup brown rice	1 cup Pico de Gallo

Marinate chicken strips 4 to 6 hours in seasoning. Make Pico de Gallo by mixing chopped onions, tomatoes, and cilantro with lemon juice and salt to taste.

Sauté marinated chicken strips with sliced onion and pepper. Cook brown rice, adding a small amount of the seasoning to the water. Serve chicken mixture over rice, topped with Pico de Gallo.

Exercise Focus for Today

Thirty minutes of resistance training using dumbbells or exercise tubing for squats, lunges, bicep curls, crunches, etc. Also do push-ups, sit-ups, pull-ups, etc.

Don't forget to chart your food consumption and exercise for the day!

Day 10

Caring for Your Spiritual Heart

Spiritual Energy In

Diet

Bible Reading: Psalm 23

Meditate on the following questions, and write your answers in the space provided.

1. Reflect on the implications for your spiritual health provided in Psalm 23.

_____

_____

2. Reflect on the implications for your soul health—your mind, will, and emotions—provided in Psalm 23.

_____

_____

3. Reflect on the implications for your physical health provided in Psalm 23.

_____

_____

Spiritual Energy Out

Exercise

Worship Exercise: Involve your whole being in worship by:
- Spending a few moments in silence.
- Focusing your mind on words that describe God's character, such as, *God is love, God is holy, God is near,* etc.

- Speaking or singing the words that describe God's character as they come into your mind.

Prayer Focus: As you use the HAND model of prayer this week, allow the pointer finger to remind you to pray for God's guidance. God is willing to give more than you are prepared to receive. Ask God to help you be sensitive to His leadership in your life and to be able to recognize His direction.

Caring for Your Physical Heart

Diet

Breakfast 1 cup cooked oatmeal with skim milk

¼ cup dried fruit, 1 cup strawberries, or ½ cup other berries

Snack Raw veggies

Lunch Tomato stuffed with tuna salad on a bed of greens (see Day 2)

Snack 1 piece of fresh fruit

Dinner 4 oz. grilled or baked fish fillet, seasoned to taste

1 cup fresh cooked green beans with slivered almonds

Salad with mixed greens and assorted raw vegetables

2 tbsp. oil and vinegar dressing

1 dinner roll

Snack ½ cup sherbet

Exercise Focus for Today

Thirty minutes of interval walking.

Don't forget to chart your food consumption and exercise for the day!

 **Day 11**

Caring for Your Spiritual Heart

Spiritual Energy In

Diet

Bible Reading: Philippians 1

Meditate on the following questions, and write your answers in the space provided.

1. What do you think it meant to Paul to be a "bond-servant of Christ Jesus," and what does it mean to you?

_____

_____

2. Why did Paul always pray that people would have "grace" and "peace"?

_____

_____

3. What are some of the transformations God has begun in your life that He will bring to completion?

_____

_____

Spiritual Energy Out

Exercise

Worship Exercise: Worship God as the Perfecter of your life, who completes what He starts.

Prayer Focus: As you continue to focus this week on the HAND model of prayer, allow the tall finger to remind you to pray for your leaders. Here's a way you can develop a prayer list of leaders at various levels of your life.

My Spiritual Leaders	Leaders in My Family	My Educational Leaders	My Civil Leaders (Government)	My Workplace Leaders (Bosses)

Caring for Your Physical Heart

Diet

Breakfast   Egg white omelet with 3 egg whites, 1 tbsp. shredded fat-free cheese, and 1 tbsp. meatless bacon bits

1 slice toast

Snack   1 stick mozzarella string cheese

Lunch   No-fat-added tuna salad: Toss together 3 oz. water-packed tuna, $\frac{1}{2}$ chopped tomato, 1 tbsp. lemon juice, 1 tbsp. chopped green onion, and a pinch of salt. Serve on a bed of greens or wrapped in a large lettuce leaf.

8 small low-fat crackers

Snack   Raw veggies

Dinner   4 oz. grilled chicken breast marinated in Italian salad dressing

Whole baked tomato sprinkled with parmesan or goat cheese

Spinach salad: Toss together 2 cups fresh spinach, $\frac{1}{2}$ cup blueberries or $\frac{1}{4}$ cup raisins or other dried fruit, 1 tbsp. gorgonzola cheese, 1 tbsp. toasted slivered almonds, 2 tbsp. vinaigrette salad dressing.

1 dinner roll

Snack   1 piece of fresh fruit

Exercise Focus for Today

Thirty minutes of walking or cardio workout video.

Don't forget to chart your food consumption and exercise for the day!

 **Day 12**

Caring for Your Spiritual Heart

Spiritual Energy In

Diet

Bible Reading: Philippians 2

Meditate on the following questions, and write your answers in the space provided.

1. How can you strike the proper balance between self-focus and focus on the interests of others?

_____

_____

2. How do you think your health is improved by discovering and walking in a balance between yourself and others?

_____

_____

3. Write out the deepest desires of your life, the things that God might be "willing" through you.

_____

_____

Spiritual Energy Out

Exercise

Worship Exercise: Philippians 2:5–11 is thought to be written in the form of a hymn. Write some free verse, rhyming poetry, or other expression of praise to Christ, and sing or speak it back to Him.

Preparation: "Sifting"

Prayer Focus: Continue to use the HAND model to guide your prayer. Today let your ring finger remind you to pray for your family members. Here are some categories that might guide your time of prayer:

- Pray for the salvation of any family members who have not received Christ as their personal Savior.
- Pray for God's peace to rule in their spirits, souls, and bodies.
- Pray for God's protection for your loved ones in spirit, soul, and body.
- Pray for God's provision for their spiritual, emotional, mental, and physical needs.
- Pray for God's providence for your family members—the unobstructed working of His perfect will in each of their lives.

Caring for Your Physical Heart

Diet

Breakfast   1 cup cereal with skim milk

¼ cup dried fruit, 1 cup strawberries, or ½ cup other berries

6 oz. low-sodium vegetable juice

Snack   1 cup nonfat yogurt (plain or with fruit)

¼ cup low-fat crunchy cereal or granola

Lunch   2 turkey roll-ups: Mix 1 tbsp. low-fat cream cheese, 2 to 3 spinach leaves, 2 oz. sliced turkey, 4 thin cucumber slices. Spread on a whole-wheat tortilla.

Snack   1 piece of fresh fruit

Dinner   Marinated and grilled flank steak (serves 4): Marinate (up to 24 hours) 1 lb. flank steak in ⅓ cup dry red cooking wine, ½ cup chopped sweet onion, 1 tbsp. soy sauce, and 3 cloves garlic, minced. Grill marinated meat to desired tenderness.

1 serving corn and black bean side*

Salad with mixed greens and assorted raw vegetables

2 tbsp. oil and vinegar dressing

Snack   ½ cup instant pudding made with skim or low-fat milk

*Corn and Black Bean Side (serves 4)

⅓ cup chopped red onion
2 to 4 tbsp. chopped cilantro
2 to 3 tbsp. lemon juice

1 cup sweet corn, fresh or canned (drained)
1 cup canned black beans, drained and rinsed
1 cup chopped red pepper

Mix together all ingredients. Serve chilled.

Exercise Focus for Today

Thirty minutes of resistance training with dumbbells, etc.

Don't forget to chart your food consumption and exercise for the day!

 **Day 13**

Caring for Your Spiritual Heart

Spiritual Energy In

Diet

Bible Reading: Philippians 3:1–21

Meditate on the following questions, and write your answers in the space provided.

1. What do you think is the difference between positive self-confidence and negative confidence in the flesh?

_____

_____

2. What was Paul's supreme life goal?

_____

_____

3. What was Paul willing to do to attain his life goal?

_____

_____

Spiritual Energy Out

Exercise

Worship Exercise: Worship God as the Giver of purpose for your life.

Prayer Focus: Your little finger on the HAND prayer model is a reminder to pray for people in need—those in poverty, distress, crisis, oppression, etc. Let the Holy Spirit guide you in praying specific things for them.

Caring for Your Physical Heart

Diet

Breakfast	2 eggs
	1 slice toast
	1 piece of fresh fruit
Snack	8 small low-fat crackers
Lunch	Mixed green salad with assorted raw vegetables and leftover flank steak or chunks of 3 oz. turkey, chicken, or tuna, 2 tbsp. oil and vinegar dressing
Snack	1 high-fiber granola or protein bar
Dinner	4 oz. fish fillet sautéed in trans fat–free margarine and drizzled with lemon juice
	1 cup vegetable medley sauté: Sauté a variety of fresh vegetables (e.g., peppers, onions, squash, snow peas) in olive oil and seasonings of your choice.
	Green salad with assorted raw vegetables
	2 tbsp. oil and vinegar dressing
Snack	1 piece of fresh fruit

Exercise Focus for Today

Thirty minutes of walking, core training, and stretching.

Don't forget to chart your food consumption and exercise for the day!

 **Day 14**

Caring for Your Spiritual Heart

Spiritual Energy In

Diet

Bible Reading: Philippians 4

Meditate on the following questions, and write your answers in the space provided.

1. How do your social relationships affect your personal health?

_____

_____

2. The word *gentle* means mild, patient, forbearing, and gracious. If this is not the natural bent of your personality, how can you begin to demonstrate a gentle spirit?

_____

_____

3. What cures anxiety?

_____

_____

Spiritual Energy Out

Exercise

Worship Exercise: Focus your worship on verses 10–13. Worship God as the all-sufficient One.

Prayer Focus: List the "impossible" challenges personally before you today in your family, school, job, community, nation, and world. Ask God to meet your "impossible" needs at every level.

Caring for Your Physical Heart

Diet

Breakfast	1 cup cereal with skim milk
	1 cup strawberries or 1 small banana
	6 oz. low-sodium vegetable juice
Snack	1 piece of fresh fruit
Lunch	Tuna salad sandwich: 3 oz. water-packed tuna, chopped tomato and green onion as desired, 1 tsp. lemon juice, 2 tbsp. light mayonnaise
Snack	Raw veggies
Dinner	4 oz. beef tenderloin fillet, seasoned and grilled to taste
	½ cup cooked green beans with slivered almonds
	1 serving fake-out mashed potatoes*
Snack	1 frozen fruit bar

*Fake-Out Mashed Potatoes (serves 4)

1 head cauliflower broken into florets   Butter substitute
¼ to ½ cup skim milk   Low-fat sour cream (optional)

Steam cauliflower until soft. Blend in food processor, adding milk until cauliflower reaches the consistency of mashed potatoes. Add butter substitute, salt, and pepper to taste. Serve with a dollop of low-fat sour cream, if desired.

Exercise: Option—Resting Day, or . . .

Thirty minutes of walking, biking, or circuit training.

Don't forget to chart your food consumption and exercise for the day!

 **Day 15**

Caring for Your Spiritual Heart

Spiritual Energy In

Diet

Bible Reading: Psalm 103
 Meditate on the following questions, and write your answers in the space provided.

1. The word *bless* comes from a Hebrew word meaning "to kneel," so it refers to adoring God. Why should you adore God?

2. Your whole soul is to be involved in adoring God. How can you adore God with your mind, will, and emotions?

3. Focus on verses 8–13, and write down what their truths mean to you personally.

Spiritual Energy Out

Exercise

Worship Exercise: The word *lovingkindness* means extraordinary, unwavering, and steadfast love and mercy. Worship God for His lovingkindness extended to you in specific situations.

Prayer Focus: Consider the things you've done for which you feel guilt and shame. Confess them to God, then claim the promises of verses 8–13, based on Christ's atonement for you.

Caring for Your Physical Heart

Diet

Breakfast	1 cup cereal with skim milk
	¼ cup dried fruit, 1 cup strawberries, or 1 small sliced banana
Snack	½ cup low-fat cottage cheese
	½ cup diced pineapple, fresh or canned in its own juice
Lunch	Chicken Caesar salad with parmesan cheese: On a bed of romaine lettuce, layer 3 oz. chunked white chicken, 1 tbsp. parmesan cheese, 2 tbsp. Caesar salad dressing, 1 tbsp. fat-free croutons.
Snack	1 piece of fresh fruit
Dinner	4 oz. roasted pork tenderloin, seasoned to taste
	1 serving baked sweet potato wedges*
	½ cup steamed snow peas with slivered almonds
Snack	½ cup instant pudding made with skim or low-fat milk

*Baked Sweet Potato Wedges (serves 4)

Cut two large sweet potatoes lengthwise into wedges, leaving the skin on. Sprinkle with substitute butter, salt, and other spices to taste (curry, tarragon, thyme). Bake thirty minutes at 375 degrees or until brown and cooked through.

Exercise Focus for Today

Thirty minutes of walking, core training, and stretching.

Don't forget to chart your food consumption and exercise for the day!

 **Day 16**

Caring for Your Spiritual Heart

Spiritual Energy In

Diet

Bible Reading: Hebrews 11:1–22

Meditate on the following questions, and write your answers in the space provided.

1. Reflect on the definition of faith given in Hebrews 11:1. In your own words, write out what this verse means to you.

_____

_____

2. Why do you think the particular people listed as heroes of faith in this passage were chosen?

_____

_____

3. Why was faith so important for them?

_____

_____

Spiritual Energy Out

Exercise

Worship Exercise: Faith is trust, and you can only have faith in someone who is trustworthy. Worship God today as the Trustworthy One.

Prayer Focus: For the next few days, we will use the Model Prayer (the Lord's Prayer) given by Jesus in Matthew 6 as a guide for praying. Pray it all the way through today, allowing the Lord to guide you in its various elements.

Caring for Your Physical Heart

Diet

Breakfast Smoothie (see Day 2)

Snack 1 stick mozzarella string cheese

Lunch 1 cup low-fat, low-sodium soup (e.g., Healthy Choice, Campbell's Healthy Request)

4 small low-fat crackers

1 slice low-fat cheese

Snack Raw veggies

Dinner 4 oz. grilled chicken breast marinated in Italian salad dressing

Whole baked tomato sprinkled with parmesan or goat cheese

Spinach salad: Toss together 2 cups fresh spinach, ½ cup blueberries or ¼ cup raisins or other dried fruit, 1 tbsp. gorgonzola cheese, 1 tbsp. toasted slivered almonds, 2 tbsp. vinaigrette salad dressing

1 dinner roll

Snack 1 piece of fresh fruit

Exercise Focus for Today

Thirty minutes of resistance training with dumbbells, exercise tubing for squats, lunges, bicep curls, crunches, etc. Or do push-ups, sit-ups, pull-ups, etc.

Don't forget to chart your food consumption and exercise for the day!

 **Day 17**

Caring for Your Spiritual Heart

Spiritual Energy In

Diet

Bible Reading: Hebrews 11:23–40

Meditate on the following questions, and write your answers in the space provided.

1. According to this passage, what motivated Moses to press forward in faith?

_____

_____

2. Verse 29 states that the people walked through the Red Sea "as though they were passing through dry land." How does faith help you walk through difficult, challenging, and even dangerous places?

_____

_____

3. What are some of the "seas" you're trusting God to "part" in your pursuit of Total Heart Health?

_____

_____

Spiritual Energy Out

Exercise

Worship Exercise: Each man and woman of faith was carrying out some element of God's great plan of redemption. Worship God for giving hope and purpose to people throughout history and to you personally.

Prayer Focus: Continue to use the Model Prayer as a guide for praying. Today, focus on the Fatherhood of God.

Caring for Your Physical Heart

Diet

Breakfast	Omelet with 2 eggs, 1 oz. nonfat cheese, 2 oz. turkey, chopped green pepper, and mushrooms
	1 piece of fresh fruit
Snack	Raw veggies
Lunch	Chicken salad: Toss together 4 oz. white chicken meat, ¼ cup sliced grapes, 1 tbsp. toasted chopped pecans, 1 tsp. lemon juice, 1 tbsp. fat-free plain yogurt. Serve on a bed of greens or wrap in a large lettuce leaf.
Snack	1 piece of fresh fruit
Dinner	Taco salad in baked tortilla bowl (see Day 5)
Snack	½ cup instant pudding made with skim or low-fat milk

Exercise Focus for Today

Thirty minutes of interval walking.

Don't forget to chart your food consumption and exercise for the day!

 **Day 18**

Caring for Your Spiritual Heart

Spiritual Energy In

Diet

Bible Reading: Hebrews 12:1–17

Meditate on the following questions, and write your answers in the space provided.

1. What are the encumbrances that weigh you down and the sins that entangle you as you pursue spiritual heart health?

_____

_____

2. What are the encumbrances that weigh you down and the sins that entangle you as you pursue a healthy mind, emotions, and will?

_____

_____

3. What are the encumbrances that weigh you down and the sins that entangle you as you pursue a healthy physical lifestyle?

_____

_____

Spiritual Energy Out

Exercise

Worship Exercise: Read verse 2 carefully. Worship Jesus for being the example you can follow in every situation. Consider the many ways His death on the cross set an example, and thank Him for being the Model in each case.

Prayer Focus: Continuing with the Model Prayer of Jesus, today zero in on the phrase, "who art in heaven."

Caring for Your Physical Heart

Diet

Breakfast	1 cup cereal with skim milk
	1 piece of fresh fruit
Snack	2 lettuce and turkey wraps (see Day 4)
Lunch	Shrimp Salad: 4 oz. cooked shrimp served with cocktail sauce and lemon juice on a bed of greens.
	8 small low-fat crackers
Snack	1 piece of fresh fruit
Dinner	1 roasted Cornish game hen, seasoned to taste
	1 serving braised cauliflower with capers (see Day 4)
	1 medium baked sweet potato, plain or with fat-free spread
Snack	1 cup nonfat yogurt (plain or with fruit)
	¼ cup low-fat crunchy cereal or granola

Exercise Focus for Today

Thirty minutes of walking or cardio workout video.

Don't forget to chart your food consumption and exercise for the day!

Day 19

Caring for Your Spiritual Heart

Spiritual Energy In

Diet

Bible Reading: Psalm 37:1–22

Meditate on the following questions, and write your answers in the space provided.

1. In God's scheme of things—the only one that matters—what really endures?

_____

_____

2. To "delight," in the Hebrew language of the Old Testament, means to find so much happiness in some activity that you want to do it all the time. How do the things in which you take delight compare with delighting yourself "in the Lord"? What changes, if any, do you need to make?

_____

_____

3. Read verse 5. How does the truth revealed here relate to the 90-Day Total Heart Health Challenge in which you are involved?

_____

_____

Spiritual Energy Out

Exercise

Worship Exercise: There are four actions listed in verses 3–7 that we are to take in our relationship with God:

73

- Trust in the Lord.
- Delight in the Lord.
- Commit your way (daily living) to the Lord.
- Rest in the Lord.

In your worship time today:
- Contemplate the fact that He is the totality of your life and being,
- Express your trust in Him,
- Express the fact that He is your delight,
- Praise Him that you can commit all your ways to Him, and
- Rest in Him for all things.

Prayer Focus: Today, focus on Jesus' words in the Model Prayer: "hallowed be Thy name." Remember, to "hallow" means to mark something as holy, special, and in a category by itself, reserved exclusively for God.

Caring for Your Physical Heart

Diet

Breakfast   1 cup cereal with skim milk

$\frac{1}{4}$ cup dried fruit, 1 cup strawberries, or $\frac{1}{2}$ cup other berries

6 oz. low-sodium vegetable juice

Snack   Raw veggies

Lunch   Tomato stuffed with tuna salad on a bed of greens (see Day 2)

Snack   1 piece of fresh fruit

Dinner   1 serving beef and broccoli sauté (see Day 2)

$\frac{1}{2}$ cup brown rice, steamed or cooked in water

Salad with mixed greens and assorted raw vegetables

2 tbsp. oil and vinegar dressing

Snack $\frac{1}{2}$ cup sherbet

Exercise Focus for Today

Thirty minutes of resistance training with dumbbells, etc.

Don't forget to chart your food consumption and exercise for the day!

 **Day 20**

Caring for Your Spiritual Heart

Spiritual Energy In

Diet

Bible Reading: Psalm 37:23–40

Meditate on the following questions, and write your answers in the space provided.

1. Consider verse 23, and compare it with Proverbs 3:5–6. Reflect on how God is establishing new "steps"—a new lifestyle—in your heart.

_____

_____

2. What changes are you beginning to see in your lifestyle?

_____

_____

3. List all of the promises found in Psalm 37:23–40 for those in a personal relationship with God through Christ.

_____

_____

Spiritual Energy Out

Exercise

Worship Exercise: List all the items in Psalm 37:23–40 that describe the love and goodness of the Lord. Then express them to the Lord, by praying, "Lord, You are (name the attribute) . . ."

Prayer Focus: Today center your prayer on the words from Jesus' Model Prayer, "Thy kingdom come." Read Romans 14:17, Matthew 24:14, and Matthew 28:18–20, and use those passages as a basis for praying for the advance of God's kingdom in the world.

Caring for Your Physical Heart

Diet

Breakfast	Open-faced turkey and cheese melt (see Day 3)
Snack	½ cup low-fat cottage cheese
	½ cup fresh or canned pineapple in its own juice
Lunch	1 serving shredded chicken salad with cranberries (see Day 3)
Snack	1 piece of fresh fruit
Dinner	4 oz. roasted pork tenderloin
	½ cup brown rice, steamed or cooked in water or broth
	1 cup steamed broccoli florets
	½ cup steamed or boiled carrot slices
Snack	½ cup fat-free frozen yogurt

Exercise Focus for Today

Thirty minutes of walking or biking.

Don't forget to chart your food consumption and exercise for the day!

Day 21

Caring for Your Spiritual Heart

Spiritual Energy In

Diet

Bible Reading: Numbers 13

Meditate on the following questions, and write your answers in the space provided.

1. As you complete today's Total Heart Challenge, you have arrived at the end of the first 21-day period. How is your situation like that of the Israelites as they stood at the edge of the promised land?

_____

_____

2. As you peer over into the next phase of the Total Heart Health Challenge, what "giants" do you see?

_____

_____

3. What does this passage teach you about your attitude and expectations as you go forward in the 90-Day Total Heart Challenge?

_____

_____

Spiritual Energy Out

Exercise

Worship Exercise: Read 1 John 4:4 and worship God for His might and overcoming power working in you.

Prayer Focus: Continuing with Jesus' Model Prayer, center your praying on the phrase, "Thy will be done on earth as it is in heaven."

Caring for Your Physical Heart

Diet

Breakfast	2 eggs
	1 slice toast
Snack	1 piece of fresh fruit
Lunch	No-fat-added tuna salad (see Day 11)
	8 small low-fat crackers
Snack	2 oz. pretzels
Dinner	4 oz. baked or broiled salmon marinated in teriyaki sauce
	1 cup vegetable medley sauté (see Day 3)
	½ cup brown rice steamed or boiled in water or broth
Snack	1 piece of fresh fruit

Exercise: Option—Resting Day, or . .

Thirty minutes of circuit training.

Don't forget to chart your food consumption and exercise for the day!

Working It Out: "Kneading"

Congratulations! You have completed the first "lap" of the 90-Day Total Heart Health Challenge. Now you begin a new level of the process that will transform your lifestyle to one focused on Total Heart Health. Using the analogy of baking bread, the first 21 days were the "sifting" phase. The goal now is to "knead in" new practices, to work them into your life until they become your new lifestyle. Keep up the good work, because you are on your way to Total Heart Health!

Objective:
To work new habits into your life
until they become a lifestyle.

Guide:
Do the following each day as designated,
for the next 19 days.

 **Day 22**

Caring for Your Spiritual Heart

Spiritual Energy In

In this phase, you will begin spiritual journaling. In the first 21 days, we provided the opportunity for you to respond briefly to questions related to the Bible passages. Now you will take your meditation on God's Word to a deeper level through journaling. Use the journal pages provided in this workbook, or purchase your own journal or notebook. Some people like to use journals published specifically for Scripture meditation, while others use a plain notebook. Here are some suggestions to guide you in your journaling:

- Note the context of the passage, the situation, and the audience at the time the text was written. (To understand and interpret Scripture properly, context is essential.)
- Write out key phrases and those on which you are focusing in your own words.
- Jot down the major themes of the passage.
- Write down your thoughts on how the context, themes, truths, and principles apply to your life both now and in the future.

Diet
Bible Reading: 1 John 1:1–2:6
   Journal today on one or more of the following topics:

1. The testimony of your experience with Christ as if you were a newspaper reporter rather than an essayist

2. The relationship between walking in God's light and living in fellowship with other followers of Christ

3. The implications of Christ as your Advocate or "defense attorney"

Spiritual Energy Out

Exercise

Worship Exercise: Think about the ways God is changing your life. Worship Him for bringing transformation to you.

Prayer Focus: Focus today on Jesus' words in the Model Prayer, "Give us this day our daily bread."

Caring for Your Physical Heart

Diet

Choose from the menus recommended in the first 21 days.

Exercise Focus for Today

(Now we're going to pick up the pace. However, if you're not ready, maintain the pace of the first 21 days.)

Forty-five minutes of an aerobic class at your church or a fitness center, followed by stretching.

Don't forget to chart your food consumption and exercise for the day!

Day 23

Caring for Your Spiritual Heart

Spiritual Energy In

Diet

Bible Reading: 1 John 2:7–29

Journal today on one or more of the following topics:

1. In light of the teachings you have just read about love, consider how you balance opposition to those with evil lifestyles who are harming themselves and others, and the mandate to love.

2. Focus on verses 15–17 and compare them to John 3:16. How are these passages related?

3. Consider verses 20–29, which speak of God's "anointing," or empowerment, in a person's life. What has God empowered you to do that reveals Jesus Christ to people and advances God's kingdom of righteousness, peace, and joy in the Holy Spirit?

Spiritual Energy Out

Exercise

Worship Exercise: Meditate on what it means that Jesus Christ is the Light of the world. Imagine what the world would be like if there were no spiritual and moral light to pierce the deep darkness of evil. Worship God as the Light-Giver.

Prayer Focus: Focus on the phrase "forgive us our trespasses as we forgive those who trespass against us."

Caring for Your Physical Heart

Diet

Choose from the menus recommended in the first 21 days.

Exercise Focus for Today

Thirty minutes of fast walking, plus thirty minutes lifting weights, targeting the upper body.

**Don't forget to chart your food consumption
and exercise for the day!**

Day 24

Caring for Your Spiritual Heart

Spiritual Energy In

Diet

Bible Reading: 1 John 3

Journal today on one or more of the following topics:

1. Consider verse 1. How does a sincere disciple of Jesus Christ, who must also live and work in the world, relate to the world?

2. Meditate on verses 2–3. Journal your thoughts on what it means that those who focus and meditate on Christ purify themselves.

3. The verb tenses in verse 9 indicate continuing action. Those in Christ may sometimes sin, but they are not characterized by lifestyles of continual sinning. How does this reveal the difference between mere religion and a genuine relationship with Christ?

4. Look at verse 23. Journal your thoughts about "His commandment."

Spiritual Energy Out

Exercise

Worship Exercise: Compose a poem, hymn, or letter to God expressing gratitude for His life, light, and love. Read, sing, or speak back to God what you have written down.

Prayer Focus: Focus on Jesus' words in the Model Prayer, "Lead us not into temptation."

Caring for Your Physical Heart

Diet

Choose from the menus recommended in the first 21 days.

Exercise Focus for Today

Forty-five minutes on an elliptical trainer, followed by stretching.

Don't forget to chart your food consumption and exercise for the day!

Day 25

Caring for Your Spiritual Heart

Spiritual Energy In

Diet

Bible Reading: 1 John 4
    Journal today on one or more of the following topics:

1. What are the implications of confessing that "Jesus Christ has come in the flesh" (verse 2)? Compare with John 1:14, John 3:16, and Philippians 2:5–11.

2. Reflect on the various types of love: friendship love, erotic love, etc. What is distinctive about the love described in verse 10?

3. How do you think love proves the existence of God, as verse 12 could imply?

Spiritual Energy Out

Exercise

Worship Exercise: Who is the person who has shown you God's love most clearly? Worship God for placing people like that in the world and for filling them with His love.

Prayer Focus: Focus today on the phrase "Deliver us from evil."

Caring for Your Physical Heart

Diet

Choose from the menus recommended in the first 21 days.

Exercise Focus for Today

Thirty minutes on a stationary bike, plus thirty minutes lifting weights and circuit training, targeting the lower body.

Don't forget to chart your food consumption and exercise for the day!

 **Day 26**

Caring for Your Spiritual Heart

Spiritual Energy In

Diet

Bible Reading: 1 John 5

Journal today on one or more of the following topics:

1. Verse 1 says it's impossible to love God the Father without loving His Child. What does this mean in the context of today's culture of tolerance and inclusiveness?

2. Read verses 4–5. What does it mean to "overcome the world," and how does a person do that? Include 1 John 2:16 in your meditation on this topic.

3. Look at verse 8. In what ways do "the Spirit and the water and the blood" confirm the truth about Jesus and His ministry?

Spiritual Energy Out

Exercise

Worship Exercise: Listen to your favorite worship album, including the song that ministers to you the most. Why does that particular song stir your love for God? Tell Him why.

Prayer Focus: Pray the phrase, "For Thine is the kingdom, and the power, and the glory, forever."

Caring for Your Physical Heart

Diet

Choose from the menus recommended in the first 21 days.

Exercise Focus for Today

Forty-five minutes of kickboxing class, followed by stretching.

**Don't forget to chart your food consumption
and exercise for the day!**

Day 27

Caring for Your Spiritual Heart

Spiritual Energy In

Diet

Bible Reading: 1 Corinthians 13

Journal today on one or more of the following topics:

1. How are noisy gongs and clanging cymbals like religious deeds performed without love?

2. Focus on verses 4–7, and list the characteristics of the genuine love given by God.

3. Why is love the greatest and most enduring of the attributes of faith, hope, and love?

Spiritual Energy Out

Exercise

Worship Exercise: Aside from the sacrifice of Jesus Christ, what is the most loving thing anyone ever did for you? Affirm to God that such a gracious blessing could not have come to you apart from His love, and worship Him for the very fact that love—the essence of His character—is in the world.

Prayer Focus: Refer to Psalm 1. Compose a prayer for the favorite person in your life, based on this psalm.

Caring for Your Physical Heart

Diet

Choose from the menus recommended in the first 21 days.

Exercise Focus for Today

Thirty minutes of fast walking.

Don't forget to chart your food consumption and exercise for the day!

Day 28

Caring for Your Spiritual Heart

Spiritual Energy In

Diet

Bible Reading: Matthew 5:1–20

Journal today on one or more of the following topics:

1. Focus on verses 1–12. The word *blessed* means "happy" and "to be congratulated." How does happiness in God's kingdom contrast with that of the world's fallen cultures and their expectations?

2. Look at verse 13. How are Christ's people who are living in the world like salt on a serving of food?

3. Read verse 17. What did Jesus mean when He said He had fulfilled the Law?

Spiritual Energy Out

Exercise

Worship Exercise: Read Acts 16:23–34. Try to understand the joy of the Philippian jailer, and express praise and worship to God appropriate to the goodness received.

Prayer Focus: Use Psalm 2 as a guide for praying today for the nations of the world. Focus especially on verse 8.

Caring for Your Physical Heart

Diet

Choose from the menus recommended in the first 21 days.

Exercise Focus for Today

Forty-five minutes of resistance training using dumbbells or exercise tubing for squats, lunges, bicep curls, crunches, etc., or push-ups, sit-ups, pull-ups, etc.

**Don't forget to chart your food consumption
and exercise for the day!**

Day 29

Caring for Your Spiritual Heart

Spiritual Energy In

Diet

Bible Reading: Matthew 5:21–48

Journal today on one or more of the following topics:

1. Read verses 21–30. What does this passage teach you about God's grace?

2. Focus on verses 39–42. What does "second-mile faith" mean to you?

3. Consider verses 43–47. What are actions and situations that would begin to stretch you as you seek to behave in a Christlike manner?

4. Think about verse 48. Is this an impossible goal?

Spiritual Energy Out

Exercise

Worship Exercise: Today we begin to worship based on the names of God.[2] There are two categories of God's Hebrew names that are included here and in the exercises that follow, the personal and the descriptive, which designate some aspect of God's character or actions.

- Worship God today by His name *El Shaddai*.
- Pronunciation: EL shad-DAI
- Meaning: "God the Almighty One"
- Key Scripture: Genesis 17:1–2[3]

Prayer Focus: Work Psalm 3 into a prayer relevant to your current life situation or to that of someone you know who needs such a prayer.

Caring for Your Physical Heart

Diet

Choose from the menus recommended in the first 21 days.

Exercise: Option—Resting Day, or . . .

Interval walking and traveling lunges (i.e. walk moderately 1 minute, walk fast for 2 minutes, then moderately 2 minutes). Then continue into traveling lunges for 1 minute. (Five minute circuit—try to do it 6 or 7 times before cooling down.)

Don't forget to chart your food consumption and exercise for the day!

 **Day 30**

Caring for Your Spiritual Heart

Spiritual Energy In

Diet

Bible Reading: Matthew 6:16–24

Journal today on one or more of the following topics:

1. Summarize Jesus' direction regarding fasting and tell why you think He spoke as He did.

2. Read verses 19–21. Consider the statement, "We value what we do, and we do what we value." What do your daily schedule and priorities say about your true values, and how do they need to change?

3. Look at verses 22–23. What are the elements that distort a person's view of God and obscure understanding of His truth?

Spiritual Energy Out

Exercise

Worship Exercise:
- Worship God today by His name *El Elyon*.
- Pronunciation: EL el-YOHN
- Meaning: "God the Most High"
- Key Scripture: Daniel 4:34

Prayer Focus: Use Psalm 4 today as a prayer guide.

Caring for Your Physical Heart

Diet

Choose from the menus recommended in the first 21 days.

Exercise Focus for Today

Forty-five minutes of an aerobic class, followed by stretching.

Don't forget to chart your food consumption and exercise for the day!

Day 31

Caring for Your Spiritual Heart

Spiritual Energy In

Diet

Bible Reading: Matthew 6:24–34

Journal today on one or more of the following topics:

1. The importance of choosing the right priorities

2. How a person's priorities should be arranged

3. How focusing on God's priorities cures anxiety

Spiritual Energy Out

Exercise

Worship Exercise:

- Worship God today by His name *Yahweh Shammah*.
- Pronunciation: yah-WEH SHAM-ah
- Meaning: "The Lord Is There"
- Key Scripture: Ezekiel 48:35

Prayer Focus: Use Psalm 5 as a guide for praying. Intercede for the salvation of the wicked.

Caring for Your Physical Heart

Diet

Choose from the menus recommended in the first 21 days.

Exercise Focus for Today

Thirty minutes of fast walking, plus thirty minutes of lifting weights, targeting the upper body.

Don't forget to chart your food consumption and exercise for the day!

Day 32

Caring for Your Spiritual Heart

Spiritual Energy In

Diet

Bible Reading: Matthew 7:1–28

Journal today on one or more of the following topics:

1. Contemplate the differences between judging and discerning.

2. Think about prayer from God's perspective as the loving Father.

3. Consider verses 15–23 in the light of Galatians 5:22–23.

Spiritual Energy Out

Exercise

Worship Exercise:
- Worship God by His name *El Olam*.
- Pronunciation: El o-LAM
- Meaning: "The Everlasting or Eternal God"
- Key Scripture: Genesis 21:32–33

Prayer Focus: Use Psalm 6 as a basis for prayer, especially interceding for hurting people, as well as yourself.

Caring for Your Physical Heart

Diet

Choose from the menus recommended in the first 21 days.

Exercise Focus for Today

Forty-five minutes on an elliptical trainer, followed by stretching.

**Don't forget to chart your food consumption
and exercise for the day!**

Day 33

Caring for Your Spiritual Heart

Spiritual Energy In

Diet

Bible Reading: Ephesians 1:1–23

Journal today on one or more of the following topics:

1. Meditate on what it means to be "chosen" in Christ.

2. How do you bring praise to the glory of His grace (verse 6)?

3. Look at verse 13 and write your thoughts on what it means to be "sealed in Him with the Holy Spirit of promise."

Spiritual Energy Out

Exercise

Worship Exercise:
- Worship the Lord today by His name *Yahweh Yireh*.
- Pronunciation: yah-WEH yir-EH
- Meaning: "The Lord Will Provide"
- Key Scripture: Genesis 22:13–14

Prayer Focus: Use Psalm 103 as a guide for praying today.

Caring for Your Physical Heart

Diet

Choose from the menus recommended in the first 21 days.

Exercise Focus for Today

Thirty minutes on a stationary bike, plus thirty minutes of lifting weights and circuit training, targeting the lower body.

**Don't forget to chart your food consumption
and exercise for the day!**

Day 34

Caring for Your Spiritual Heart

Spiritual Energy In

Diet

Bible Reading: Ephesians 2:1–22

Journal today on one or more of the following topics:

1. Think about verses 1–2. How were you "dead in your trespasses and sins" before you received Christ?

2. What does it mean to you to be God's "workmanship" (verse 10)?

3. What does it mean to you that you are a "dwelling of God in the Spirit" (verse 22)?

Spiritual Energy Out

Exercise

Worship Exercise:
- Worship God today by focusing on His name *Magen*.
- Pronunciation: ma-GAIN
- Meaning: "Dwelling Place, Refuge, Fortress"
- Key Scripture: Psalm 91:1–2

Prayer Focus: Use Psalm 91 as a prayer guide.

Caring for Your Physical Heart

Diet

Choose from the menus recommended in the first 21 days.

Exercise Focus for Today

Forty-five minutes of kickboxing class, followed by stretching.

Don't forget to chart your food consumption and exercise for the day!

 **Day 35**

Caring for Your Spiritual Heart

Spiritual Energy In

Diet

Bible Reading: Ephesians 3:1–21
  Journal today on one or more of the following topics:

  1. In what ways are you a "steward" of God's grace (see verse 2)?

  2. Consider verse 6. Why would it have been shocking to Paul's original readers
     to learn that God's salvation included the Gentiles, and what does that mean to
     you now?

  3. Meditate on verse 17, and what it means to be "rooted and grounded in love."

Spiritual Energy Out

Exercise

Worship Exercise:
  • Worship God today as *Qedosh Yisrael.*
  • Pronunciation: ke-DOSH yis-ra-AIL
  • Meaning: "The Holy One of Israel"
  • Key Scripture: Leviticus 19:1–2

Prayer Focus: Use Psalm 139 as a guide for praying today.

Caring for Your Physical Heart

Diet

Choose from the menus recommended in the first 21 days.

Exercise Focus for Today

Thirty minutes of fast walking.

**Don't forget to chart your food consumption
and exercise for the day!**

 **Day 36**

Caring for Your Spiritual Heart

Spiritual Energy In

Diet

Bible Reading: Ephesians 4:1–32

Journal today on one or more of the following topics:

1. Consider verse 2 and some of the ways you can show tolerance "in love" to other people in your church.

2. In light of verse 14, what are ways we behave childishly and are led along into error?

3. Who are the people to whom you need to speak constructive words, and what should you say to them (verse 29)?

Spiritual Energy Out

Exercise

Worship Exercise:
- Worship God today based on His name *Adonai.*
- Pronunciation: a-do-NAI
- Meaning: "Lord, Master"
- Key Scripture: Psalm 16:2

Prayer Focus: Use Psalm 78:1–8 as a guide for interceding today for your family.

Caring for Your Physical Heart

Diet

Choose from the menus recommended in the first 21 days.

Exercise Focus for Today

Resistance training with dumbbells, etc.

Don't forget to chart your food consumption and exercise for the day!

 **Day 37**

Caring for Your Spiritual Heart

Spiritual Energy In

Diet

Bible Reading: Ephesians 5:1–33

Journal today on one or more of the following topics:

1. In light of verse 4, how could your speech and routine conversation be improved to bring more glory to Christ?

2. Think about verses 11–12, and how contemporary culture relishes "unfruitful deeds of darkness."

3. Meditate on verse 18 and how people substitute intoxicants, medications, foods, and other elements to try to get the stimulus provided by the fullness of the Holy Spirit.

Spiritual Energy Out

Exercise

Worship Exercise:
- Worship God as *Melek*.
- Pronunciation: ME-lek
- Meaning: "King"
- Key Scripture: Psalm 72:1–3

Prayer Focus: Use Psalm 72 as a prayer guide today.

Caring for Your Physical Heart

Diet

Choose from the menus recommended in the first 21 days.

Exercise: Option—Resting Day, or . . .

Twenty minutes of biking along with a Pilates class at your local fitness or community center.

Don't forget to chart your food consumption and exercise for the day!

 **Day 38**

Caring for Your Spiritual Heart

Spiritual Energy In

Diet

Bible Reading: Ephesians 6:1–24

Journal today on one or more of the following topics:

1. How should you honor your parents (even if they have not lived honorable lives), and what do you think are the results of doing so?

2. Read verses 10–17, and think about each component of God's spiritual armor in relation to your life and daily experience.

3. Consider what it means to "pray . . . in the Spirit" (verse 18). Be quiet, and seek to allow the Holy Spirit to form His prayer in you; then write it down, and pray it back to God.

Spiritual Energy Out

Exercise

Worship Exercise:
- Worship God today as *Yahweh Rophe*.
- Pronunciation: yah-WEH ro-FEH
- Meaning: "The Lord Who Heals"
- Key Scripture: Exodus 15:26

Prayer Focus: Use Psalm 102 to pray for those who are sick, afflicted, or in some other way experiencing a crisis, as well as yourself.

Caring for Your Physical Heart

Diet

Choose from the menus recommended in the first 21 days.

Exercise Focus for Today

Forty-five minutes of an aerobic class, followed by stretching.

Don't forget to chart your food consumption and exercise for the day!

Day 39

Caring for Your Spiritual Heart

Spiritual Energy In

Diet

Bible Reading: Isaiah 53:1–12

Journal today on one or more of the following topics:

1. How did Jesus Christ differ from the assumptions the Pharisees and others had made about the coming Messiah? How does He differ from assumptions people make about Him today?

2. Why was it necessary for Christ to suffer for our sins? (Hint: Refer to Romans 6:23.)

3. Meditate on verse 10 and write down what you think it means.

Spiritual Energy Out

Exercise

Worship Exercise:
- Worship God today by His name *El Chay*.
- Pronunciation: EL CHAY
- Meaning: "The God Who Lives"
- Key Scripture: 2 Kings 19:15–16

Prayer Focus: Use Psalm 90 as a prayer guide today.

Caring for Your Physical Heart

Diet

Choose from the menus recommended in the first 21 days.

Exercise Focus for Today

Thirty minutes of fast walking, plus thirty minutes of lifting weights, targeting the upper body.

Don't forget to chart your food consumption and exercise for the day!

 **Day 40**

Caring for Your Spiritual Heart

Spiritual Energy In

Diet

Bible Reading: Romans 5:1–21

Journal today on one or more of the following topics:

1. What is "peace with God," and how do you get it?

2. Meditate on verses 3–5. In what way can trials and tribulations actually be productive in a person's life?

3. Why did God give the Law? What is grace, and why is it necessary?

Spiritual Energy Out

Exercise

Worship Exercise:
- Worship God today by His name *Yahweh Shalom.*
- Pronunciation: yah-WEH sha-LOME
- Meaning: "The Lord Is Peace"
- Key Scripture: Judges 6:24

Prayer Focus: Use Psalm 112 to guide your praying today.

Caring for Your Physical Heart

Diet

Choose from the menus recommended in the first 21 days.

Exercise Focus for Today

Forty-five minutes on an elliptical trainer, followed by stretching.

Don't forget to chart your food consumption and exercise for the day!

DAYS 41–90

Becoming Who You Were
Meant to Be: "Baking"

Congratulations! You have progressed through the first 40 days of your Total Heart Health Challenge. Now you move forward into a new phase. In the Bible, "40 years" symbolized the passing of one generation and the beginning of another. In our bread-making analogy, you have "sifted" (Days 1–21), "kneaded" (Days 22–40), and now you are going to "bake." The focus in this phase will be to solidify your new spiritual and physical practices into a lifestyle, leading to continuing transformation and a consistent way of living that will contribute to Total Heart Health.

We now add a ministry action challenge, listing some suggested service projects in which you can become involved. Select one or several, and then put them into practice!

Possible Ministry Projects

- Volunteer for your church's hospital team.
- Be a prayer volunteer.
- Visit nursing homes.
- Give time as a volunteer at a rescue mission.
- Serve a crisis pregnancy center.
- Minister to elderly and shut-ins.
- Teach a class.

- Volunteer to help clean the church.
- Teach English to non-English speakers.
- Minister to women in prison and/or their families.
- Volunteer regularly in the church nursery.

You get the idea!

Objective:
To solidify the new habits and undergo consistent transformation toward Total Heart Health.

Guide:
Do the following each day as designated, for the next 50 days.

Day 41

Caring for Your Spiritual Heart

Spiritual Energy In

Diet
Bible Reading: Esther 1:1–22
  Journal using the following outline:

1. The background (context) of this passage

2. The central truth of this passage

3. How the central truth of this passage relates to you and your present experience

Spiritual Energy Out

Exercise
Worship Exercise: We now begin a period of worshiping God centered on His attributes, which refer to His perfections, or the elements of His holy character. We will list some of the Bible passages listing specific attributes. However, keep in mind that the whole of Scripture reveals God's character, and that Jesus Christ is the "Living Word," the ultimate revelation of what God is like.

- Worship God today for His aseity as The Self-Existent One.
- Meaning: Self-existence (You and I are the result of a previous cause, but there is nothing before God to "cause" Him to exist.)
- Key Scripture: Isaiah 44:6

Prayer Focus: In previous weeks, you focused your worship on the names of God. Now, in this period, we will use Psalm 23 as a prayer guide, because the actions and works of God expressed there demonstrate the practical reality of many of His names for us.

- Focus: "The LORD is my Shepherd" (Ps. 23:1)
- Name of God: *Yahweh Roi* (Shepherd)

Ministry Action(s): Ask the Lord to guide you in choosing from the list on pages 121–122 or to give you another project to undertake.

Caring for Your Physical Heart

Diet

Choose from the menus recommended in the first 21 days.

Exercise Focus for Today

Thirty minutes on a stationary bike, plus thirty minutes lifting weights and circuit training, targeting the lower body.

Don't forget to chart your food consumption and exercise for the day!

 **Day 42**

Caring for Your Spiritual Heart

Spiritual Energy In

Diet

Bible Reading: Esther 2:1–23
   Journal using the following outline:

   1. The background (context) of this passage

   2. The central truth of this passage

   3. How the central truth of this passage relates to you and your present experience

Spiritual Energy Out

Exercise

Worship Exercise

   • Worship God as The Compassionate One
   • Key Scripture: Exodus 34:6–7

Prayer Focus: Psalm 23

   • Focus: "I shall not want" (Ps. 23:1)
   • Name of God: *Yahweh Yireh* (The LORD Will Provide)

Ministry Action(s): Ask the Lord to guide you in choosing a ministry action from the list on pages 121–122 or to give you another project to undertake.

Caring for Your Physical Heart

Diet

Choose from the menus recommended in the first 21 days.

Exercise Focus for Today

Forty-five minutes of kickboxing class, followed by stretching.

Don't forget to chart your food consumption and exercise for the day!

Day 43

Caring for Your Spiritual Heart

Spiritual Energy In

Diet

Bible Reading: Esther 3:1–15

  Journal using the following outline:

  1. The background (context) of this passage

  2. The central truth of this passage

  3. How the central truth of this passage relates to you and your present experience

Spiritual Energy Out

Exercise

Worship Exercise:

- Worship God as The Gracious One
- Key Scripture: Exodus 34:6–7

Prayer Focus: Psalm 23

- Focus: "He makes me lie down in green pastures" (Ps. 23:2)
- Name of God: *Yahweh Shalom* (The LORD Is Peace)

Ministry Action(s): Ask the Lord to guide you in selecting a ministry action from the list on pages 121–122 or to give you another project to undertake.

Caring for Your Physical Heart

Diet

Choose from the menus recommended in the first 21 days.

Exercise Focus for Today

Try a spinning or cycling class at your local fitness center.

**Don't forget to chart your food consumption
and exercise for the day!**

 **Day 44**

Caring for Your Spiritual Heart

Spiritual Energy In

Diet

Bible Reading: Esther 4:1–17

  Journal using the following outline:

    1. The background (context) of this passage

    2. The central truth of this passage

    3. How the central truth of this passage relates to you and your present experience

Spiritual Energy Out

Exercise

Worship Exercise:

- Worship God today as The One Who Is Slow to Anger
- Key Scripture: Exodus 34:6–7

Prayer Focus: Psalm 23

- Focus: "He leads me beside quiet waters" (Ps. 23:2)
- Names of God: *Yahweh Roi, Yahweh Shalom* (The LORD Is My Shepherd, The LORD Is My Peace)

Ministry Action(s): Ask the Lord to guide you in choosing a ministry option from the list on pages 121–122 or to give you another ministry idea.

Caring for Your Physical Heart

Diet

Choose from the menus recommended in the first 21 days.

Exercise: Option—Resting Day, or . . .

Thirty minutes of fast walking, followed by core training and stretching.

Don't forget to chart your food consumption and exercise for the day!

 **Day 45**

Caring for Your Spiritual Heart

Spiritual Energy In

Diet

Bible Reading: Esther 5:1–14
  Journal using the following outline:

  1. The background (context) of this passage

  2. The central truth of this passage

  3. How the central truth of this passage relates to you and your present experience

Spiritual Energy Out

Exercise

Worship Exercise:

- Worship God today as The One Who Is Lovingkind.
- Key Scripture: Exodus 34:6–7

Prayer Focus: Psalm 23

- Focus: "He restores my soul" (Ps. 23:3)
- Name of God: *Yahweh Rophe* (The LORD Who Heals)

Ministry Action(s): Ask the Lord to guide you in choosing from the suggestions listed on pages 121–122 or to give you another ministry idea.

Caring for Your Physical Heart

Diet

Choose from the menus recommended in the first 21 days.

Exercise Focus for Today

Forty-five minutes of aerobic class, followed by stretching.

Don't forget to chart your food consumption and exercise for the day!

Day 46

Caring for Your Spiritual Heart

Spiritual Energy In

Diet

Bible Reading: Esther 6:1–14

Journal by the following outline:

1. The background (context) of this passage

2. The central truth of this passage

3. How the central truth of this passage relates to you and your present experience

Spiritual Energy Out

Exercise

Worship Exercise:

- Worship God as The One Who Is Truth
- Key Scripture: Exodus 34:6–7

Prayer Focus: Psalm 23

- Focus: "He guides me in the paths of righteousness For His name's sake" (Ps. 23:3)
- Name of God: *Yahweh Tsidkenu (zid-KAY-nu)* (The LORD Our Righteousness)

Ministry Action(s): Ask the Lord to guide you in choosing a ministry from the list on pages 121–122 or to give you another ministry idea.

Caring for Your Physical Heart

Diet

Choose from the menus recommended in the first 21 days.

Exercise Focus for Today

Thirty minutes of fast walking, plus thirty minutes of lifting weights, targeting the upper body.

Don't forget to chart your food consumption and exercise for the day!

Day 47

Caring for Your Spiritual Heart

Spiritual Energy In

Diet

Bible Reading: Esther 7:1–10

Journal using the following outline:

1. The background (context) of this passage

2. The central truth of this passage

3. How the central truth of this passage relates to you and your present experience

Spiritual Energy Out

Exercise

Worship Exercise:

- Worship God as The One Who Forgives
- Key Scripture: Exodus 34:6–7

Prayer Focus: Psalm 23

- Focus: "Even though I walk through the valley of the shadow of death, I fear no evil, for You are with me; Your rod and Your staff, they comfort me" (Ps. 23:4)
- Name of God: *Yahweh Shammah* (The LORD Who Is There)

Ministry Action(s): Ask the Lord to guide you in choosing from the ministry list on pages 121–122 or to give you another ministry idea.

Caring for Your Physical Heart

Diet

Choose from the menus recommended in the first 21 days.

Exercise Focus for Today

Forty-five minutes on an elliptical trainer, followed by stretching.

Don't forget to chart your food consumption and exercise for the day!

Day 48

Caring for Your Spiritual Heart

Spiritual Energy In

Diet

Bible Reading: Esther 8:1–17
  Journal using the following outline:

1. The background (context) of this passage

2. The central truth of this passage

3. How the central truth of this passage relates to you and your present experience

Spiritual Energy Out

Exercise

Worship Exercise:

- Worship God as The Immutable (Unchangeable) One
- Key Scripture: Psalm 102:26–27

Prayer Focus: Psalm 23

- Focus: "You prepare a table before me in the presence of my enemies" (Ps. 23:5)
- Name of God: *Yahweh Maon* (*Ma-ohn*) (The LORD My Refuge and Strong Tower)

Ministry Action(s): Ask God's guidance in choosing from the suggested ministry actions listed on pages 121–122 or to give you another ministry idea.

Caring for Your Physical Heart

Diet

Choose from the menus recommended in the first 21 days.

Exercise Focus for Today

Thirty minutes on a stationary bike, plus thirty minutes lifting weights and circuit training, targeting the lower body.

Don't forget to chart your food consumption and exercise for the day!

 **Day 49**

Caring for Your Spiritual Heart

Spiritual Energy In

Diet

Bible Reading: Esther 9:1–19

Journal using the following outline:

1. The background (context) of this passage

2. The central truth of this passage

3. How the central truth of this passage relates to you and your present experience

Spiritual Energy Out

Exercise

Worship Exercise:

- Worship God as The Everywhere-Present (Omnipresent) One
- Key Scripture: Proverbs 15:3

Prayer Focus: Psalm 23

- Focus: "You have anointed my head with oil; My cup overflows" (Ps. 23:5)
- Name (Title) of God: *Ruach (ROO-ak)* (Spirit)

Ministry Action(s): Ask God to guide you in choosing a ministry action from the list on pages 121–122 or to give you another project to undertake.

Caring for Your Physical Heart

Diet

Choose from the menus recommended in the first 21 days.

Exercise Focus for Today

Forty-five minutes of kickboxing class, followed by stretching.

Don't forget to chart your food consumption and exercise for the day!

Day 50

Caring for Your Spiritual Heart

Spiritual Energy In

Diet

Bible Reading: Esther 9:20–10:3
  Journal using the following outline:

  1. The background (context) of this passage

  2. The central truth of this passage

  3. How the central truth of this passage relates to you and your present experience

Spiritual Energy Out

Exercise

Worship Exercise:

- Worship God as The All-Knowing (Omniscient) One
- Key Scripture: 1 John 3:20

Prayer Focus: Psalm 23

- Focus: "Surely goodness and lovingkindness will follow me all the days of my life, And I will dwell in the house of the LORD forever" (Ps. 23:6)
- Name of God: *Miqweh Yisrael* (*MIK-weh*) (The Hope of Israel)

Ministry Action(s): Ask God to guide you in making a ministry action choice from the list on pages 121–122 or to give you another ministry idea.

Caring for Your Physical Heart

Diet

Choose from the menus recommended in the first 21 days.

Exercise Focus for Today

Thirty minutes of fast walking.

Don't forget to chart your food consumption and exercise for the day!

 **Day 51**

Caring for Your Spiritual Heart

Spiritual Energy In

Diet

Bible Reading: Psalm 34:1–22
   Journal by the following outline:

   1. The background (context) of this passage

   2. The central truth of this passage

   3. How the central truth of this passage relates to you and your present experience

Spiritual Energy Out

Exercise

Worship Exercise:

- Worship God as The All-Powerful (Omnipotent) One
- Key Scripture: Matthew 28:18

Prayer Focus: You have completed praying through Psalm 23. Now we will turn to a great prayer of Jesus, found in John 17, and use it as a guide for our own intercessions.

- Focus: John 17:1–12
- As you meditate on this passage, allow the Holy Spirit to direct you to other intercession needs.

Ministry Action(s): Ask God to help you choose a ministry action from the list on pages 121–122 or to give you another ministry idea.

Caring for Your Physical Heart

Diet

Choose from the menus recommended in the first 21 days.

Exercise: Option—Resting Day, or . . .

Twenty minutes of walking or biking, followed by a Pilates class or video.

Don't forget to chart your food consumption and exercise for the day!

 **Day 52**

Caring for Your Spiritual Heart

Spiritual Energy In

Diet

Bible Reading: James 1:1–27
    Journal using the following outline:

1. The background (context) of this passage

2. The central truth of this passage

3. How the central truth of this passage relates to you and your present experience

Spiritual Energy Out

Exercise

Worship Exercise:

- Worship God as The All-Wise One
- Key Scripture: Isaiah 11:2

Prayer Focus: John 17

- Pray based on John 17:13–21.
- Allow the Holy Spirit to lead you to pray for other related matters.

Ministry Action(s): Ask the Lord to guide you in choosing a ministry option from the list on pages 121–122 or to give you another idea.

Caring for Your Physical Heart

Diet

Choose from the menus recommended in the first 21 days.

Exercise Focus for Today

Forty-five minutes of an aerobic class, followed by stretching.

Don't forget to chart your food consumption and exercise for the day!

Day 53

Caring for Your Spiritual Heart

Spiritual Energy In

Diet

Bible Reading: James 2:1–26

   Journal using the following outline:

1. The background (context) of this passage

2. The central truth of this passage

3. How the central truth of this passage relates to you and your present experience

Spiritual Energy Out

Exercise

Worship Exercise:

- Worship God as The One with All Understanding
- Key Scripture: Isaiah 11:2

Prayer Focus: John 17

- Pray based on John 17:22–26.
- Allow the Holy Spirit to lead you in praying for other related matters.

Ministry Action(s): Ask the Lord to guide you in choosing from the ministry options on pages 121–122 or to give you another idea.

Caring for Your Physical Heart

Diet

Choose from the menus recommended in the first 21 days.

Exercise Focus for Today

Thirty minutes of fast walking, plus thirty minutes of lifting weights, targeting the upper body.

**Don't forget to chart your food consumption
and exercise for the day!**

Day 54

Caring for Your Spiritual Heart

Spiritual Energy In

Diet

Bible Reading: James 3:1–18
   Journal using the following outline:

   1. The background (context) of this passage

   2. The central truth of this passage

   3. How the central truth of this passage relates to you and your present experience

Spiritual Energy Out

Exercise

Worship Exercise:

- Worship God as The Counselor
- Key Scripture: Isaiah 11:2

Prayer Focus: Pray using the S.E.L.F. and HAND models.

Ministry Action(s): Ask the Lord to guide you in choosing from the ministry options on pages 121–122 or to give you another idea.

Caring for Your Physical Heart

Diet

Choose from the menus recommended in the first 21 days.

Exercise Focus for Today

Forty-five minutes on an elliptical trainer, followed by stretching.

Don't forget to chart your food consumption and exercise for the day!

Day 55

Caring for Your Spiritual Heart

Spiritual Energy In

Diet

Bible Reading: James 4:1–17

Journal using the following outline:

1. The background (context) of this passage

2. The central truth of this passage

3. How the central truth of this passage relates to you and your present experience

Spiritual Energy Out

Exercise

Worship Exercise:

- Worship God as The One With All Strength
- Key Scripture: Isaiah 11:2

Prayer Focus: Use the S.E.L.F. and HAND models.

Ministry Action(s): Ask the Lord to guide you in choosing from the options listed on pages 121–122 or to give you another ministry idea.

Caring for Your Physical Heart

Diet

Choose from the menus recommended in the first 21 days.

Exercise Focus for Today

Thirty minutes on a stationary bike, plus thirty minutes of lifting weights and circuit training, targeting the lower body.

Don't forget to chart your food consumption and exercise for the day!

 **Day 56**

Caring for Your Spiritual Heart

Spiritual Energy In

Diet

Bible Reading: James 5:1–20
  Journal using the following outline:

  1. The background (context) of this passage

  2. The central truth of this passage

  3. How the central truth of this passage relates to you and your present experience

Spiritual Energy Out

Exercise

Worship Exercise:

- Worship God as The One With All Knowledge
- Key Scripture: Isaiah 11:2

Prayer Focus: Continue using the S.E.L.F. and HAND models.

Ministry Action(s): Ask the Lord to lead you in choosing from the ministry options listed on pages 121–122 or to give you another idea.

Caring for Your Physical Heart

Diet

Choose from the menus recommended in the first 21 days.

Exercise Focus for Today

Forty-five minutes of kickboxing class, followed by stretching.

Don't forget to chart your food consumption and exercise for the day!

Day 57

Caring for Your Spiritual Heart

Spiritual Energy In

Diet

Bible Reading: Psalm 51:1–19
  Journal using the following outline:

  1. The background (context) of this passage

  2. The central truth of this passage

  3. How the central truth of this passage relates to you and your present experience

Spiritual Energy Out

Exercise

Worship Exercise:

- Worship God as The Sovereign Ruler of All
- Key Scripture: 1 Chronicles 29:11

Prayer Focus: Pray using the S.E.L.F. and HAND models.

Ministry Action(s): Ask the Lord to guide you in choosing from the ministry list on pages 121–122 or to give you another idea.

Caring for Your Physical Heart

Diet

Choose from the menus recommended in the first 21 days.

Exercise Focus for Today

Thirty minutes of fast walking. Try long intervals—2 minutes moderate, 2 minutes hard, 2 minutes moderate, etc.

**Don't forget to chart your food consumption
and exercise for the day!**

Day 58

Caring for Your Spiritual Heart

Spiritual Energy In

Diet

Bible Reading: Matthew 13:1–30
  Journal using the following outline:

1. The background (context) of this passage

2. The central truth of this passage

3. How the central truth of this passage relates to you and your present experience

Spiritual Energy Out

Exercise

Worship Exercise: Exodus 15:1–11

- Pray or sing this song to the Lord, adapting it to your life and contemporary times.

Prayer Focus: We will now focus on Psalm 119, the Bible's longest chapter. It is divided into sections based on the Hebrew alphabet. We will pray through this great psalm one section at a time.

- Pray through the *Aleph* section (verses 1–8) in your own words.

Ministry Action(s): Ask the Lord to guide you in choosing from the ministry options on pages 121–122 or to give you another idea.

Caring for Your Physical Heart

Diet

Choose from the menus recommended in the first 21 days.

Exercise: Option—Resting Day, or . . .

Twenty minutes biking or walking, followed by a Pilates class or video.

Don't forget to chart your food consumption and exercise for the day!

Day 59

Caring for Your Spiritual Heart

Spiritual Energy In

Diet

Bible Reading: Matthew 13:31–58
   Journal using the following outline:

1. The background (context) of this passage

2. The central truth of this passage

3. How the central truth of this passage relates to you and your present experience

Spiritual Energy Out

Exercise

Worship Exercise: Judges 5:1–5

- Pray or sing this song to the Lord, adapting it to your life and contemporary times.

Prayer Focus: Psalm 119:9–16

Ministry Action(s): Ask the Lord to guide you in choosing from the ministry options listed on pages 121–122 or to give you another idea.

Caring for Your Physical Heart

Diet

Choose from the menus recommended in the first 21 days.

Exercise Focus for Today

Forty-five minutes of an aerobic class, followed by stretching.

**Don't forget to chart your food consumption
and exercise for the day!**

Day 60

Caring for Your Spiritual Heart

Spiritual Energy In

Diet

Bible Reading: Psalm 19:1–14
  Journal using the following outline:

1. The background (context) of this passage

2. The central truth of this passage

3. How the central truth of this passage relates to you and your present experience

Spiritual Energy Out

Exercise

Worship Exercise: Revelation 5:9–14

• Pray or sing this worship song to the Lord, relating it to your life and contemporary times.

Prayer Focus: Psalm 119:17–24

Ministry Action(s): Ask the Lord to guide you in choosing from the ministry options listed on pages 121–122 or to give you another idea.

Caring for Your Physical Heart

Diet

Choose from the menus recommended in the first 21 days.

Exercise Focus for Today

Thirty minutes of fast walking, plus thirty minutes lifting weights, targeting the upper body.

Don't forget to chart your food consumption and exercise for the day!

 **Day 61**

Caring for Your Spiritual Heart

Spiritual Energy In

Diet

Bible Reading: Romans 8:1–17
 Journal by the following outline:

 1. The background (context) of this passage

 2. The central truth of this passage

 3. How the central truth of this passage relates to you and your present experience

Spiritual Energy Out

Exercise

Worship Exercise: Deuteronomy 32

 • Study the Song of Moses in Deuteronomy 32, and use it as a guide for your personal worship today, speaking or singing pertinent portions to the Lord.

Prayer Focus: Psalm 119:25–32

Ministry Action(s): Ask the Lord to guide you in choosing from the ministry options listed on pages 121–122 or to give you another idea.

Caring for Your Physical Heart

Diet

Choose from the menus recommended in the first 21 days.

Exercise Focus for Today

Forty-five minutes on an elliptical trainer, followed by stretching.

Don't forget to chart your food consumption and exercise for the day!

 **Day 62**

Caring for Your Spiritual Heart

Spiritual Energy In

Diet

Bible Reading: Romans 8:18–39

Journal using the following outline:

1. The background (context) of this passage

2. The central truth of this passage

3. How the central truth of this passage relates to you and your present experience

Spiritual Energy Out

Exercise

Worship Exercise: 2 Samuel 22

- Meditate on David's song in this passage, and use it as a guide for your worship, speaking or singing pertinent sections of the song to the Lord.

Prayer Focus: Psalm 119:33–40

Ministry Action(s): Ask the Lord to guide you in choosing from the ministry options listed on pages 121–122 or to give you another idea.

Caring for Your Physical Heart

Diet

Choose from the menus recommended in the first 21 days.

Exercise Focus for Today

Thirty minutes on a stationary bike, plus thirty minutes lifting weights, targeting the lower body.

**Don't forget to chart your food consumption
and exercise for the day!**

Day 63

Caring for Your Spiritual Heart

Spiritual Energy In

Diet

Bible Reading: Psalm 139:1–24

Journal by the following outline:

1. The background (context) of this passage

2. The central truth of this passage

3. How the central truth of this passage relates to you and your present experience

Spiritual Energy Out

Exercise

Worship Exercise: Psalm 45

- Speak or sing this song to the Lord as the Holy Spirit directs you.

Prayer Focus: Psalm 119:41–48

Ministry Action(s): Ask the Lord to guide you in choosing from the ministry options listed on pages 121–122 or to give you another idea.

Caring for Your Physical Heart

Diet
Choose from the menus recommended in the first 21 days.

Exercise Focus for Today
Forty-five minutes of kickboxing class, followed by stretching.

**Don't forget to chart your food consumption
and exercise for the day!**

 **Day 64**

Caring for Your Spiritual Heart

Spiritual Energy In

Diet

Bible Reading: John 12:1–11
  Journal using the following outline:

1. The background (context) of this passage

2. The central truth of this passage

3. How the central truth of this passage relates to you and your present experience

Spiritual Energy Out

Exercise

Worship Exercise: Psalm 46

- Speak or sing this song to the Lord, adapting it to your personal experience and contemporary times.

Prayer Focus: Psalm 119:49–56

Ministry Action(s): Ask the Lord to guide you in choosing from the ministry options listed on pages 121–122 or to give you another idea.

Caring for Your Physical Heart

Diet

Choose from the menus recommended in the first 21 days.

Exercise Focus for Today

Do interval walking. Begin by warming up, then 1 minute moderate walking, 2 minutes faster, 1 minute moderate, 1 minute traveling lunges, then cooldown.

Don't forget to chart your food consumption and exercise for the day!

 **Day 65**

Caring for Your Spiritual Heart

Spiritual Energy In

Diet

Bible Reading: 1 Peter 1:1–12
  Journal using the following outline:

  1. The background (context) of this passage

  2. The central truth of this passage

  3. How the central truth of this passage relates to you and your present experience

Spiritual Energy Out

Exercise

Worship Exercise: Psalm 68

- Use the thoughts expressed in this psalm as a song you can speak or sing to the Lord.

Prayer Focus: Psalm 119:57–64

Ministry Action(s): Ask the Lord to guide you in choosing from the ministry options listed on pages 121–122 or to give you another idea.

Caring for Your Physical Heart

Diet

Choose from the menus recommended in the first 21 days.

Exercise: Option—Resting Day, or . . .

Twenty minutes of biking, followed by a Pilates class or video.

Don't forget to chart your food consumption and exercise for the day!

 **Day 66**

Caring for Your Spiritual Heart

Spiritual Energy In

Diet

Bible Reading: 1 Peter 1:13–25
  Journal using the following outline:

1. The background (context) of this passage

2. The central truth of this passage

3. How the central truth of this passage relates to you and your present experience

Spiritual Energy Out

Exercise

Worship Exercise: Psalm 75

- Using the thoughts in this psalm, compose a praise song that you can speak or sing to the Lord.

Prayer Focus: Psalm 119:65–72

Ministry Action(s): Ask the Lord to guide you in choosing from the ministry options listed on pages 121–122 or to give you another idea.

Caring for Your Physical Heart

Diet

Choose from the menus recommended in the first 21 days.

Exercise Focus for Today

Forty-five minutes of an aerobic class, followed by stretching.

Don't forget to chart your food consumption and exercise for the day!

Day 67

Caring for Your Spiritual Heart

Spiritual Energy In

Diet

Bible Reading: 1 Peter 2:1–12

   Journal using the following outline:

     1. The background (context) of this passage

     2. The central truth of this passage

     3. How the central truth of this passage relates to you and your present experience

Spiritual Energy Out

Exercise

Worship Exercise: Psalm 87

- Use the thoughts in this passage to compose a praise song to the Lord that you can speak or sing to Him.

Prayer Focus: Psalm 119:73–80

Ministry Action(s): Ask the Lord to guide you in choosing from the ministry options on pages 121–122 or to give you another idea.

Caring for Your Physical Heart

Diet

Choose from the menus recommended in the first 21 days.

Exercise Focus for Today

Thirty minutes of fast walking, plus thirty minutes lifting weights, targeting the upper body.

Don't forget to chart your food consumption and exercise for the day!

 **Day 68**

Caring for Your Spiritual Heart

Spiritual Energy In

Diet

Bible Reading: 1 Peter 2:13–25
   Journal using the following outline:

   1. The background (context) of this passage

   2. The central truth of this passage

   3. How the central truth of this passage relates to you and your present experience

Spiritual Energy Out

Exercise

Worship Exercise: Psalm 92:1

• Sing or speak thoughts from this song to the Lord.

Prayer Focus: Psalm 119:81–88

Ministry Action(s): Ask the Lord to guide you in choosing from the ministry options list on pages 121–122 or to give you another idea.

Caring for Your Physical Heart

Diet

Choose from the menus recommended in the first 21 days.

Exercise Focus for Today

Forty-five minutes on an elliptical trainer, followed by stretching.

Don't forget to chart your food consumption and exercise for the day!

Day 69

Caring for Your Spiritual Heart

Spiritual Energy In

Diet

Bible Reading: 1 Peter 3:1–22
  Journal using the following outline:

  1. The background (context) of this passage

  2. The central truth of this passage

  3. How the central truth of this passage relates to you and your present experience

Spiritual Energy Out

Exercise

Worship Exercise: Psalm 108

  • Speak or sing a song to the Lord based on this passage.

Prayer Focus: Psalm 119:89–96

Ministry Action(s): Ask the Lord to guide you in choosing from the ministry options listed on pages 121–122 or to give you another idea.

Caring for Your Physical Heart

Diet

Choose from the menus recommended in the first 21 days.

Exercise Focus for Today

Thirty minutes on a stationary bike, plus thirty minutes of lifting weights and circuit training, targeting the lower body.

**Don't forget to chart your food consumption
and exercise for the day!**

 **Day 70**

Caring for Your Spiritual Heart

Spiritual Energy In

Diet

Bible Reading: 1 Peter 4:1–19

Journal your answers to the following questions:

1. What issue or need is this passage addressing?

2. What does this passage say to my heart?

3. What am I going to do about it?

Spiritual Energy Out

Exercise

Worship Exercise

- Worship Jesus Christ in His office (position of authority) of the Prophet of God
- As the Prophet, Jesus tells us what God and His kingdom are like and what He is doing among us.
- Key Scriptures: Matthew 12:18; Hebrews 1:1; Revelation 19:10

Prayer Focus: Psalm 119:97–104

Ministry Action(s): We will now focus on putting our spiritual gifts into operation. These are the abilities God gives us to serve Him by serving others. Not everyone will have the same set of spiritual gifts, but as the situation demands, God will allow us to operate in the gift that is appropriate to the ministry need, whether we normally function in that gift or not.

- Read Romans 12.
- Verse 6 identifies the gift of prophecy. This is not only the *fore*telling of the future, but it is also the *forth*telling of God's truth.
- Allow the Lord to bring to your mind someone who is hurting himself or herself and others through a destructive lifestyle, and how you can minister God's biblical truth in a positive, loving way to that person.

Caring for Your Physical Heart

Diet

Choose from the menus recommended in the first 21 days.

Exercise Focus for Today

Forty-five minutes of kickboxing class, followed by stretching.

Don't forget to chart your food consumption and exercise for the day!

Day 71

Caring for Your Spiritual Heart

Spiritual Energy In

Diet

Bible Reading: 1 Peter 5:1–13

Journal your answers to the following questions:

1. What issue or need is this passage addressing?

2. What does this passage say to my heart?

3. What am I going to do about it?

Spiritual Energy Out

Exercise

Worship Exercise

- Worship Jesus Christ in His office as Priest.
- As our High Priest, Jesus mediates, or represents, us before the Father and the Father to us.
- Key Scripture: Hebrews 7

Prayer Focus: Psalm 119:105–112

Ministry Action(s)

- Romans 12:6 also mentions faith, the ability to trust God.
- Today, consider a ministry action that would require a greater level of faith on your part.

Caring for Your Physical Heart

Diet

Choose from the menus recommended in the first 21 days.

Exercise Focus for Today

Forty minutes of fast walking.

Don't forget to chart your food consumption and exercise for the day!

 **Day 72**

Caring for Your Spiritual Heart

Spiritual Energy In

Diet

Bible Reading: Ecclesiastes 3:1–15
  Journal your answers to the following questions:

  1. What issue or need is this passage addressing?

  2. What does this passage say to my heart?

  3. What am I going to do about it?

Spiritual Energy Out

Exercise

Worship Exercise

- Worship Jesus Christ as King.
- Key Scripture: John 18:37

Prayer Focus: Psalm 119:113–120

Ministry Action(s)

- Romans 12:7 names service as a spiritual gift.
- The Greek word for *service* is the same word from which we get *deacon*. Among other things, it refers to those who prepare and serve food.
- Consider assisting a ministry to the hungry.

Caring for Your Physical Heart

Diet

Choose from the menus recommended in the first 21 days.

Exercise: Option—Resting Day, or . . .

Twenty minutes biking, followed by a Pilates class or video.

Don't forget to chart your food consumption and exercise for the day!

 **Day 73**

Caring for Your Spiritual Heart

Spiritual Energy In

Diet

Bible Reading: John 14:1–21

Journal your answers to the following questions:

1. What issue or need is this passage addressing?

2. What does this passage say to my heart?

3. What am I going to do about it?

Spiritual Energy Out

Exercise

Worship Exercise

- Worship God the Holy Spirit as the Personality in the Godhead who brings the ministry of Jesus (who reveals the Father) to your heart.
- Key Scriptures: John 15:26; 16:14

Prayer Focus: Psalm 119:121–128

Ministry Action(s)

- Romans 12:7 lists teaching as a spiritual gift, referring especially to the ability to help others better understand God's Word.
- You may not consider yourself a teacher, but there are those with whom you can share informally about God, such as your children, relatives, best friends, and work colleagues.

Caring for Your Physical Heart

Diet
Choose from the menus recommended in the first 21 days.

Exercise Focus for Today
Forty-five minutes of an aerobic class, followed by stretching.

Don't forget to chart your food consumption and exercise for the day!

 **Day 74**

Caring for Your Spiritual Heart

Spiritual Energy In

Diet

Bible Reading: John 15:1–27

Journal your answers to the following questions:

1. What issue or need is this passage addressing?

2. What does this passage say to my heart?

3. What am I going to do about it?

Spiritual Energy Out

Exercise

Worship Exercise

- Worship God the Holy Spirit as the One who brings you spiritual birth with God's life.
- Key Scriptures: John 3:6; 6:63

Prayer Focus: Psalm 119:129–136

Ministry Action(s)

- Romans 12:8 lists exhortation as a spiritual gift. This is the ability, given by God, to give people encouragement, as well as make them comfortable in situations where they would otherwise feel uncomfortable.

- Who in your daily circle of contacts and acquaintances needs reassurance and encouragement? Identify them and minister to them through the gift of exhortation.

Caring for Your Physical Heart

Diet
Choose from the menus recommended in the first 21 days.

Exercise Focus for Today
Thirty minutes of fast walking, plus thirty minutes of lifting weights, targeting the upper body.

Don't forget to chart your food consumption and exercise for the day!

 **Day 75**

Caring for Your Spiritual Heart

Spiritual Energy In

Diet

Bible Reading: Psalm 8:1–9
   Journal your answers to the following questions:

   1. What issue or need is this passage addressing?

   2. What does this passage say to my heart?

   3. What am I going to do about it?

Spiritual Energy Out

Exercise

Worship Exercise

- Worship God the Holy Spirit as the One who inspires and preserves the Bible, God's Word, without which you would not know the truth about God.
- Key Scripture: 2 Timothy 3:16

Prayer Focus: Psalm 119:137–144

Ministry Action(s)

- Romans 12:8 lists giving as a spiritual gift. As with the other gifts, all of us are to be givers, but there are people enabled by God to give at an unusual level of faith and generosity.

- Discover a situation that needs you to give yourself and perhaps your treasures in a selfless manner, and do it.

Caring for Your Physical Heart

Diet

Choose from the menus recommended in the first 21 days.

Exercise Focus for Today

Forty-five minutes on an elliptical trainer, followed by stretching.

Don't forget to chart your food consumption and exercise for the day!

Day 76

Caring for Your Spiritual Heart

Spiritual Energy In

Diet

Bible Reading: Romans 12:1–21

Journal your answers to the following questions:

1. What issue or need is this passage addressing?

2. What does this passage say to my heart?

3. What am I going to do about it?

Spiritual Energy Out

Exercise

Worship Exercise

- Worship God the Holy Spirit as the One who guides you.
- Key Scripture: John 15:26

Prayer Focus: Psalm 119:145–152

Ministry Action(s)

- Romans 12:8 mentions leading as a gift. To lead means to oversee something or someone, to direct it properly, not by controlling, but by serving and setting an example.
- Maybe you don't think of yourself as a leader, but there are those for whom you can provide positive guidance. Allow the Holy Spirit to use you in this role.

Caring for Your Physical Heart

Diet

Choose from the menus recommended in the first 21 days.

Exercise Focus for Today

Thirty minutes on a stationary bike, plus thirty minutes of lifting weights, targeting the lower body.

Don't forget to chart your food consumption and exercise for the day!

 **Day 77**

Caring for Your Spiritual Heart

Spiritual Energy In

Diet

Bible Reading: Psalm 95:1–11

Journal your answers to the following questions:

1. What issue or need is this passage addressing?

2. What does this passage say to my heart?

3. What am I going to do about it?

Spiritual Energy Out

Exercise

Worship Exercise

- Worship God the Holy Spirit as the One who empowers you to function in spiritual gifts, operating at a level that blesses others in a manner that would be impossible without Him.
- Key Scriptures: 1 Corinthians 12:4; Hebrews 2:4

Prayer Focus: Psalm 119:153–160

Ministry Action(s)

- Romans 12:8 lists mercy as a spiritual gift.
- Get involved in a ministry to prisoners and/or their families. Or, think of someone you consider an adversary at work or in some other relationship and plan a way to bless the individual—and then do it.

Caring for Your Physical Heart

Diet
Choose from the menus recommended in the first 21 days.

Exercise Focus for Today
Forty-five minutes of kickboxing class, followed by stretching.

Don't forget to chart your food consumption and exercise for the day!

 **Day 78**

Caring for Your Spiritual Heart

Spiritual Energy In

Diet

Bible Reading: Colossians 1:1–29

Journal your answers to the following questions:

1. What issue or need is this passage addressing?

2. What does this passage say to my heart?

3. What am I going to do about it?

Spiritual Energy Out

Exercise

Worship Exercise

- Worship God the Holy Spirit as the One who enables you to claim and declare that Jesus Christ is your Lord.
- Key Scripture: 1 Corinthians 12:3

Prayer Focus: Psalm 119:161–168

Ministry Action(s)

- Read 1 Corinthians 12.
- First Corinthians 12:8 identifies wisdom as a spiritual gift. This is the divinely given ability to bring God's truth into application in specific situations.
- Ask God to help you minister wisdom to people needing direction.

Caring for Your Physical Heart

Diet
Choose from the menus recommended in the first 21 days.

Exercise Focus for Today
Thirty minutes of fast walking, followed by core training and stretching.

**Don't forget to chart your food consumption
and exercise for the day!**

Day 79

Caring for Your Spiritual Heart

Spiritual Energy In

Diet

Bible Reading: Colossians 2:1–23

Journal your answers to the following questions:

1. What issue or need is this passage addressing?

2. What does this passage say to my heart?

3. What am I going to do about it?

Spiritual Energy Out

Exercise

Worship Exercise

- Worship God as Triune, one in three, three in one, the One who is complete.
- Consider confessing aloud The Apostles' Creed:

  I believe in God the Father Almighty; Maker of Heaven and Earth; and in Jesus Christ His only (begotten) Son our Lord; who was conceived by the Holy Ghost, born of the Virgin Mary; suffered under Pontius Pilate, was crucified, dead, and buried; He descended into hell; the third day He rose from the dead; He ascended into heaven; and sitteth at the right hand of God the Father Almighty; from thence He shall come to judge the quick and the dead. I believe in the Holy Ghost; the holy catholic Church; the communion of saints; the forgiveness of sins; the resurrection of the body; and the life everlasting. Amen.

Prayer Focus: Psalm 119:169–176

Ministry Action(s)

- First Corinthians 12:8 lists "the word of knowledge" as a spiritual gift. This is the ability to speak knowledgeably about a situation whose details you might not know naturally.
- Ask God to give you insight into situations and people so that you may pray and minister to them more effectively and point them to Christ.

Caring for Your Physical Heart

Diet

Choose from the menus recommended in the first 21 days.

Exercise: Option—Resting Day, or . . .

Twenty minutes biking followed by a Pilates class or video.

Don't forget to chart your food consumption and exercise for the day!

 **Day 80**

Caring for Your Spiritual Heart

Spiritual Energy In

Diet

Bible Reading: Colossians 3:1–25

Journal your answers to the following questions:

1. What issue or need is this passage addressing?

2. What does this passage say to my heart?

3. What am I going to do about it?

Spiritual Energy Out

Exercise

Worship Exercise: Use Psalm 84 to guide your worship.

Prayer Focus: Use Isaiah 53 as a guide for prayer, focusing on the sacrifice of Jesus and the need for people to receive His gift of eternal life.

Ministry Action(s)

- First Corinthians 12:9 mentions healing as a gift of the Holy Spirit.
- Volunteer for your church's hospital visitation ministry, and pray for sick people.

Caring for Your Physical Heart

Diet

Choose from the menus recommended in the first 21 days.

Exercise Focus for Today

Forty-five minutes of an aerobic class, followed by stretching.

Don't forget to chart your food consumption and exercise for the day!

 **Day 81**

Caring for Your Spiritual Heart

Spiritual Energy In

Diet

Bible Reading: Colossians 4:1–18
  Journal your answers to the following questions:

  1. What issue or need is this passage addressing?

  2. What does this passage say to my heart?

  3. What am I going to do about it?

Spiritual Energy Out

Exercise

Worship Exercise: Use Psalm 9 as a guide for your worship.

Prayer Focus: Use Isaiah 55 as a prayer guide.

Ministry Action(s)

- First Corinthians 12:10 names miracles as a gift of the Spirit. Miracles are deeds of unusual power, performed by the Holy Spirit and pointing people to Christ.
- Remember that the greatest miracle is helping another person be transformed by receiving Christ as his or her Savior. Allow God to use you to do something for someone that would point him or her to Jesus.

Caring for Your Physical Heart

Diet

Choose from the menus recommended in the first 21 days.

Exercise Focus for Today

Thirty minutes of fast walking, plus thirty minutes of weight lifting, targeting the upper body.

Don't forget to chart your food consumption and exercise for the day!

 **Day 82**

Caring for Your Spiritual Heart

Spiritual Energy In

Diet

Bible Reading: Romans 14:1–23
  Journal your answers to the following questions:

  1. What issue or need is this passage addressing?

  2. What does this passage say to my heart?

  3. What am I going to do about it?

Spiritual Energy Out

Exercise

Worship Exercise: Use Psalm 62 to guide your worship.

Prayer Focus: Use Isaiah 58 as a prayer guide.

Ministry Action(s)

- First Corinthians 12:10 cites distinguishing of spirits, or discernment, as a spiritual gift. This is the ability to supernaturally see the true power behind something or someone.
- Pray for God to use you to discern what is really going on around you and to help you pray for and alert people with whom you have a close relationship.

Caring for Your Physical Heart

Diet

Choose from the menus recommended in the first 21 days.

Exercise Focus for Today

Forty-five minutes on an elliptical trainer, followed by stretching.

Don't forget to chart your food consumption and exercise for the day!

Day 83

Caring for Your Spiritual Heart

Spiritual Energy In

Diet

Bible Reading: Galatians 5:1–15

   Journal your answers to the following questions:

     1. What issue or need is this passage addressing?

     2. What does this passage say to my heart?

     3. What am I going to do about it?

Spiritual Energy Out

Exercise

Worship Exercise: Use Psalm 56 as a guide for worship.

Prayer Focus: Use Isaiah 60 as a prayer guide.

Ministry Action(s)

- First Corinthians 12:10 lists "various kinds of tongues" as a gifting of the Spirit. There are many views about the nature of this gift. However, above all, it means to be able to speak to people in a language they can understand. (See Acts 2:8.)

- Ask God for the ability to speak to people in understandable language that points them to Him. For example, ask Him to help you speak the "language" of your spouse or children, or of people from a different cultural background.

Caring for Your Physical Heart

Diet

Choose from the menus recommended in the first 21 days.

Exercise Focus for Today

Thirty minutes on a stationary bike, plus thirty minutes lifting weights, targeting the lower body.

Don't forget to chart your food consumption and exercise for the day!

 **Day 84**

Caring for Your Spiritual Heart

Spiritual Energy In

Diet

Bible Reading: Galatians 5:16–26

Journal your answers to the following questions:

1. What issue or need is this passage addressing?

2. What does this passage say to my heart?

3. What am I going to do about it?

Spiritual Energy Out

Exercise

Worship Exercise: Use Psalm 87 as a guide for worship.

Prayer Focus: Use Isaiah 61 as a prayer guide, comparing it to Luke 4.

Ministry Action(s)

- First Corinthians 12:10 says that "interpretation of tongues" is a spiritual gift. This is the God-given ability to take words spoken by someone else and show their meaning in a way that builds up others. Again, there are many understandings of the meaning of this gift. The key is that it is given so that people may benefit from the speech of another.

- Ask God for the ability in your home, school, or workplace to be a person who helps people understand and benefit from one another's words.

Caring for Your Physical Heart

Diet
Choose from the menus recommended in the first 21 days.

Exercise Focus for Today
Forty-five minutes of kickboxing class, followed by stretching.

Don't forget to chart your food consumption and exercise for the day!

 **Day 85**

Caring for Your Spiritual Heart

Spiritual Energy In

Diet

Bible Reading: Psalm 96:1–13

Journal your answers to the following questions:

1. What issue or need is this passage addressing?

2. What does this passage say to my heart?

3. What am I going to do about it?

Spiritual Energy Out

Exercise

Worship Exercise: Allow Psalm 32 to guide your worship.

Prayer Focus: Use Isaiah 62 as a prayer guide.

Ministry Action(s):

- Read 1 Corinthians 13.
- Ask God to help you make love the motivation and guiding principle of the use of your spiritual gifts.
- Think of an unlovable person in your life, and ask God for an opportunity to demonstrate unconditional love to him or her.

Caring for Your Physical Heart

Diet

Choose from the menus recommended in the first 21 days.

Exercise Focus for Today

Thirty-five minutes of fast walking with intervals and traveling lunges.

Don't forget to chart your food consumption and exercise for the day!

 **Day 86**

Caring for Your Spiritual Heart

Spiritual Energy In

Diet

Bible Reading: Matthew 18:1–20

Journal your answers to the following questions:

1. What issue or need is this passage addressing?

2. What does this passage say to my heart?

3. What am I going to do about it?

Spiritual Energy Out

Exercise

Worship Exercise: Use Psalm 16 to guide your worship.

Prayer Focus: Use 2 Corinthians 4:16–18 as a prayer guide.

Ministry Action(s)

- Read Matthew 25, focusing on verses 31–46.
- Get involved in a ministry to the poor, either through your financial giving, or direct personal involvement, or both.

Caring for Your Physical Heart

Diet

Choose from the menus recommended in the first 21 days.

Exercise: Option—Resting Day, or . . .

Twenty minutes of biking followed by a Pilates class or video.

Don't forget to chart your food consumption and exercise for the day!

Day 87

Caring for Your Spiritual Heart

Spiritual Energy In

Diet

Bible Reading: Matthew 18:21–35

Journal your answers to the following questions:

1. What issue or need is this passage addressing?

2. What does this passage say to my heart?

3. What am I going to do about it?

Spiritual Energy Out

Exercise

Worship Exercise: Use Psalm 8 as a guide for worship.

Prayer Focus: Use 2 Corinthians 10:1–5 as a prayer guide.

Ministry Action(s): Matthew 25:31–46

- Find out how you can assist with ministries to the homeless, and then give them your help.

Caring for Your Physical Heart

Diet

Choose from the menus recommended in the first 21 days.

Exercise Focus for Today

Forty-five minutes of an aerobic class, followed by stretching.

Don't forget to chart your food consumption and exercise for the day!

 **Day 88**

Caring for Your Spiritual Heart

Spiritual Energy In

Diet

Bible Reading: Acts 9

Journal your answers to the following questions:

1. What issue or need is this passage addressing?

2. What does this passage say to my heart?

3. What am I going to do about it?

Spiritual Energy Out

Exercise

Worship Exercise: Use Psalm 4 to guide your worship.

Prayer Focus: Use Galatians 5:16–26 as a prayer guide.

Ministry Action(s): Matthew 25:31–46

- Sort through your clothes and give away as many of them as you can—including some of your best—to a ministry providing clothing for the needy.

Caring for Your Physical Heart

Diet

Choose from the menus recommended in the first 21 days.

Exercise Focus for Today

Thirty minutes of fast walking, plus thirty minutes lifting weights, targeting the upper body.

Don't forget to chart your food consumption and exercise for the day!

 **Day 89**

Caring for Your Spiritual Heart

Spiritual Energy In

Diet

Bible Reading: Acts 10

   Journal your answers to the following questions:

   1. What issue or need is this passage addressing?

   2. What does this passage say to my heart?

   3. What am I going to do about it?

Spiritual Energy Out

Exercise

Worship Exercise: Use Psalm 5 to guide your worship.

Prayer Focus: Pray the S.E.L.F. model all the way through to the end.

Ministry Action(s): Matthew 25:31–46

   • Find special ways to minister to sick people.

Caring for Your Physical Heart

Diet

Choose from the menus recommended in the first 21 days.

Exercise Focus for Today

Forty-five minutes on an elliptical trainer, followed by stretching.

Don't forget to chart your food consumption and exercise for the day!

Day 90

Caring for Your Spiritual Heart

Spiritual Energy In

Diet

Bible Reading: Proverbs 31:10–31
   Journal your answers to the following questions:

   1. What issue or need is this passage addressing?

   2. What does this passage say to my heart?

   3. What am I going to do about it?

Spiritual Energy Out

Exercise

Worship Exercise: Use Psalm 90 as a guide for worship.

Prayer Focus: Use the HAND model, praying it all the way through.

Ministry Action(s): Matthew 25:31–46

   • Find ways to be involved in ministering to prison inmates and their families, and
     pray especially for those in prison for the gospel's sake.

Caring for Your Physical Heart

Diet
Choose from the menus recommended in the first 21 days.

Exercise Focus for Today
Thirty minutes on a stationary bike, plus thirty minutes lifting weights, targeting the lower body

Don't forget to chart your food consumption and exercise for the day!

CONGRATULATIONS!

You have now completed our 90-Day Total Heart Health Challenge. The process was designed to help you "sift out" old destructive habits and "sift in" new healthy behaviors for your Total Heart, "knead in" the new practices, and "bake" them into a consistent lifestyle. We hope you have discovered that the new ways are now routine, and that you feel it is unusual when you don't spend at least thirty minutes a day in personal focus on the Lord, spend thirty minutes in exercise, and maintain a consistently good diet.

Remember, Total Heart Health is a lifestyle, not a short-term fad. Stay with it, and discover the rich, full, healthy life God intended for you from the beginning. We close with the blessing from 1 Thessalonians 5:23, whose theme has permeated this entire process like a fragrant perfume:

> *May the God of peace Himself*
> *sanctify you entirely;*
> *and may your*
> *spirit and soul and body*
> *be preserved complete, without blame*
> *at the coming of our Lord Jesus Christ.*

Notes

1. "How People Change: Psychological Theories and the Transtheoretical Model for Behavioral Change," The Cooper Institute, 2003.

2. For more information, see Ann Spangler, *Praying the Names of God* (Grand Rapids, MI: Zondervan, 2004).

3. All key Scriptures are those suggested in *Praying the Names of God.*

Total Heart Health Journal

_____

_____

_____

_____

_____

_____

_____

_____

_____

_____

_____

_____

_____

_____

_____

_____

_____

_____

_____

_____

_____

_____

_____

_____

_____

_____

_____

_____

_____

_____

_____

_____

_____

_____

_____

_____

_____

_____

_____

_____

_____

_____

_____

_____

_____

_____

_____

_____

Total Heart Health Journal

_____
_____
_____
_____
_____
_____
_____
_____
_____
_____
_____
_____
_____
_____
_____
_____
_____
_____
_____
_____
_____
_____
_____
_____
_____
_____
_____

Total Heart Health Journal

Total Heart Health Journal

Total Heart Health Journal

_____

_____

_____

_____

_____

_____

_____

_____

_____

_____

_____

_____

_____

_____

_____

_____

_____

_____

_____

_____

_____

_____

_____

_____

_____

_____

_____

_____

A New You in 90 Days

Ed and JoBeth Young of the Second Baptist Church of Houston along with two of the nations leading cardiologists, Michael Duncan and Richard Leachman, have developed the Total Heart Health system, a program that insures you keep a balanced focus on your physical and spiritual health with:

- ◆ Fitness Tips
- ◆ Smart Recipes
- ◆ Daily Devotions
- ◆ Tools to become your own health & fitness coach
- ◆ A 90 Day Total Heart Health Challenge
- ◆ All around strategies for better living

www.thomasnelson.com

NELSON IMPACT

W PUBLISHING GROUP

COUNTRYMAN

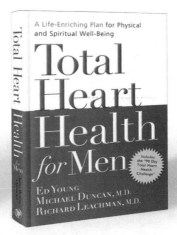

TOTAL HEART HEALTH FOR WOMEN
Hardcover • 0-8499-0012-3 • $22.99

TOTAL HEART HEALTH FOR MEN
Hardcover • 0-8499-0013-1 • $22.99

TOTAL HEART HEALTH
FOR WOMEN
WORKBOOK
Tradepaper
1-4185-0127-1
$16.99

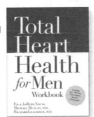

TOTAL HEART HEALTH
FOR MEN
WORKBOOK
Tradepaper
1-4185-0126-3
$16.99

365 DAYS OF
TOTAL HEART HEALTH
DEVOTIONAL
Hardcover
1-4041-0209-4
$15.99

TOTAL HEART HEALTH
POCKET PLANNER
Tradepaper*
0-8499-9862-X

*FREE with book purchase

Honor Christ Physically and Spiritually...
with your **Total Heart**

Daily Food Chart
Physical Energy In

Food
(Enter here what you actually ate, whether on the recommended diet or not.)

Breakfast

Food: _____

_____

Calories: _____

Lunch

Food: _____

_____

Calories: _____

Dinner

Food: _____

_____

Calories: _____

Snacks

Food: _____

_____

Calories: _____

TOTAL CALORIES TODAY: _____

Water
Number of 8-ounce glasses (8 recommended): _____

Vitamins/Supplements/Medications:

_____

_____

Daily Exercise Chart
Physical Energy Out

Exercise

(Be sure to warm up at the beginning of your workout and cool down at the end.)

Total time spent exercising (minimum of thirty minutes recommended):

_____

Cardiovascular Exercise
Type: _____

Time: _____

Resistance (strength) Exercise
Type: _____

Time: _____

Flexibility (stretching) Exercise
Type: _____

Time: _____

Time allowed for warm-up and cool down (very important)
Warm-up: _____

Cool down: _____

Your weight today: _____

(It is not essential to weigh daily. You may want to weigh two to three times a week. Also, be aware that weight can vary because of water retention.)